Advance Praise for *Innovation As Usual*

"The authors offer a compelling case for highly focused innovation and how leaders at all levels can become architects of an environment that makes innovation and creativity routine behavior."

—Lise Kingo, Executive Vice President, Novo Nordisk A/S

"In our changing world, business as usual is not a recipe for success. Good innovation usually is. *Innovation as Usual* inspires and suggests practical approaches to building the kind of organizational culture that encourages innovative behaviors."

—Jan Mattsson, Executive Director, UNOPS

"*Innovation as Usual* is a fabulous read that induces you to drive your team to focus, select, and persist on innovation at work. A complete hands-on book for all managers."

—Narayana Murthy, Chairman Emeritus, Infosys Limited

"A single idea can change an entire world—like containerization changed the world of transport. The future of every organization depends on its ability to invest in the plain-looking ideas that could create its own moment of containerization. This book offers a bright proposal on how to achieve that."

—Michael Pram Rasmussen, Chairman,
A.P. Møller - Mærsk A/S

"This book breathes optimism and opportunity and provides an actionable framework for creating a winning innovative environment."

—Rory Simpson, Chief Learning Officer, Telefónica Group

"This book is about an idea whose time has come. An eminently practical guide on how to convert innovative ideas into commercial success."

—Vijay Govindarajan, Professor, Tuck School of Business at Dartmouth College; bestselling author, *Reverse Innovation*

"*Innovation as Usual* shows you how to make innovation happen within your team on a regular basis. A rich and fascinating read."

—Jørgen Vig Knudstorp, CEO, The LEGO Group

"*Innovation as Usual* is packed with powerful ideas and practical advice for aspiring innovators. A great guide for people who want to make the world a better place."

—Jessica Jackley, cofounder, Kiva; venture partner, Collaborative Fund

"I've been looking for this book for a long time! *Innovation as Usual* provides an easy-to-implement process on how to organize the innovative instincts of the people in your company."

—Jacob Holm, President and CEO, Fritz Hansen A/S

"The authors challenge the notion that innovation cannot happen as part of every leader's day-to-day responsibilities. It is packed with vivid examples and great tactics to ensure a consistent execution of exciting new ideas for any leader within an organization. Great read!"

—Frans Johansson, CEO, The Medici Group; author,
The Medici Effect and *The Click Moment*

"If you are tired of reading about innovation as fluffy stuff and want to create results by doing new things, this is the book for you."

—Joergen Bardenfleth, Strategy Director, Microsoft
International; Chairman, Symbion

INNOVATION
∧
~~BUSINESS~~
AS USUAL

INNOVATION

^ ~~BUSINESS~~

AS USUAL

HOW TO HELP YOUR PEOPLE
BRING **GREAT IDEAS** TO LIFE

PADDY MILLER
THOMAS WEDELL-WEDELLSBORG

HARVARD BUSINESS REVIEW PRESS

Boston, Massachusetts

Printed in the United States of America

10 9 8 7 6 5 4 3 2 1

The web addresses referenced in this book were live and correct at the time of the book's publication but may be subject to change.

Library of Congress Cataloging-in-Publication Data

Miller, Paddy.
Innovation as usual : how to help your people bring great ideas to life / Paddy Miller and Thomas Wedell-Wedellsborg.
    pages cm
  ISBN 978-1-4221-4419-0 (alk. paper)
1. Creative ability in business. 2. Creative thinking. 3. Diffusion of innovations—Management. 4. Organizational behavior. 5. New products. I. Wedell-Wedellsborg, Thomas. II. Title.
  HD53.M549 2013
  658.4'063--dc23

                    2012041300

The paper used in this publication meets the requirements of the American National Standard for Permanence of Paper for Publications and Documents in Libraries and Archives Z39.48-1992.

To Sara and Marjorie

To Gitte and Henrik (a.k.a. mor og far)

CONTENTS

DEFINITIONS

INNOVATION

Creating results by doing new things

INNOVATION ARCHITECT

A person that makes *other* people innovate
by changing the environment they work in

INNOVATION

∧ ~~BUSINESS~~

AS USUAL

CHAPTER 1

INNOVATION AS USUAL

HOW TO CHANGE WHAT PEOPLE DO, EVERY DAY

Leaders must help their people innovate as
part of their jobs

Some years ago at a casual dinner, the conversation had turned
to the topic of innovation when one of our friends, a manager
in a big company, made an admission:

> I'm beginning to think that my people just aren't very
> innovative. They are smart people, and we all know how
> important innovation is—but at the end of the day, we just
> keep doing the same old thing we've always done. I'm not
> sure what to do about that.

This book is our response to that comment. It is a practical,
hands-on book written for managers and leaders, and it

shows how you can help your people to be more innovative so that it becomes an integrated part of their daily work. This ability—to help *other* people innovate—isn't relevant only for senior executives, but is a skill that every single manager can benefit from. Thus, this book is not aimed at CEOs and chief innovation officers, nor is it focused on special innovation units like R&D departments or corporate venture teams. Rather, it is aimed squarely at *local* leaders, fighting the good fight on the frontlines of the organization, working with the people they have and with limited time and budgets. In short, this book is about getting to what you could call *innovation as usual*: a state where your regular employees, in regular jobs like finance, marketing, sales, or operations, make innovation happen as a part of what they do every day.

Creative Choices:
The Possibility of Innovation

The starting point lies in realizing something important: innovation may seem to be an elusive phenomenon, but the *possibility* of innovation permeates our lives. Just think about it: every single day, people face the opportunity to try something new, to do something different from how they did it yesterday. Play with a new idea. Test a new tool. Try a novel tack with a client. Seek new input. Use a different management style. Change the way they have meetings. Like a shadow reality, adjacent to ours, the opportunity to innovate is with us always: every time we choose to do business as usual, we *could* equally have chosen to tweak the routines a bit and see what happens.

We call this *the creative choice*, and in a sense, it is the smallest possible building block of innovation: the act of deviating from the norm, stepping away from business as usual for a brief moment. The sentiment is perhaps best captured in the famous lines from Robert Frost's poem "The Road Not Taken":

Two roads diverged in a wood,
And I—I chose the one less traveled by
And that has made all the difference

As you read this book, you will notice that we like to use various images and metaphors to talk about innovation; we are great believers in the power of a well-chosen image to serve as a useful thinking tool, especially when talking about notoriously fuzzy topics like innovation, culture, and the like. Here, we introduce a key comparison that we use throughout the book: that of thinking of innovative behavior as a choice between two roads in a forest.

Like the person in Frost's poem, people face a choice between two roads; only for them, it's a daily choice. One is the road of business as usual, and it is a wide and well-paved road: people have traveled it often, and they know exactly where it will take them. The other option is to take the creative path—a new, bumpier, more winding road whose final destination is obscured by the trees. By and large, people overwhelmingly choose to stay on the road of business as usual, day in and day out.

The Leader as an Architect of Ideas

As a leader, it is your job to change that. More specifically, the approach we describe in this book rests on a central idea:

Your primary job as a leader is not to innovate; it is to become an innovation architect, creating a work environment that helps your people engage in the key innovation behaviors as part of their daily work.

Our approach contains three key ideas that we want to highlight. First, it emphasizes that being an innovation leader is different from being an innovator yourself. Too many leaders, whether of small teams or large companies, are obsessed with how they *themselves* can become the next creative wunderkind, generating brilliant new ideas for their business. In the pursuit of that particular pipe dream, noble as it is, they ignore the first and most basic job of a leader: to achieve great things *through other people*. Innovation leadership is not about attaining new levels of personal brilliance. It is about turning *your people* into innovators. There *are* situations where leaders can be personally innovative—see the box, "Where Can Leaders Themselves Be Innovators?"—but those are not the norm.

Where Can Leaders Themselves Be Innovators?

While this book focuses on the leader's role as an innovation architect, there are, of course, situations where leaders are well suited to be innovators themselves. The question to ask yourself is, *in what areas do you have more domain expertise than your employees?* In what areas are you the foremost expert in your company?

Part of the answer is that leaders are well suited to innovate in the domains of leadership and strategy, that is, the areas of endeavor that come naturally with being a leader:

- **Management methods.** Can you find new ways of working or leading your people? Gary Hamel and Bill Breen's book *The Future of Management* provides food for thought on this topic. Also useful is *Giant Steps in Management*, in which Julian Birkinshaw and Michael Mol provide an overview of all major innovations in the field of management.*

- **Strategy and business models.** By virtue of their position, leaders tend to have a stronger grasp than employees of their business model and the strategic landscape in which they operate. Are there new ways of creating or capturing value that you can identify? A great book on this is Constantinos Markides's *Game-Changing Strategies.*

Another part of the answer will be defined by your professional history. Fernando Val, chief operating officer of the Spanish low-cost airline Vueling, spent twelve years in the air force prior to joining the company; that in-depth immersion has given him an excellent base for generating new and useful ideas to optimize Vueling's complicated logistical puzzle.

*All the sources we mention in the book are referenced in full at the end of the book, in the Notes section.

Through *your* personal and professional past, what particular and specific domains do you understand better than others? Which worlds have you had more exposure to than your people? And what are you most passionate about?

Second, our approach focuses on making innovation happen as an integrated part of the daily work flow. Many corporate innovation efforts are trapped on what we call "Brainstorm Island": like an annual innovation vacation, people are sent on a professionally facilitated offsite meeting, spending two colorful days brainstorming for ideas. After those two exceptional, invigorating days, however, they return to a workplace where nothing has changed, and by and large, fourteen days later, pretty much everybody is back to doing business as usual. The reality is, you won't find good ideas by spending two days a year on Brainstorm Island. The pursuit of innovation should not be an exceptional event; quite the contrary, it should be *unexceptional*, something that takes place on the *other* 363 days of the year. As a leader, you have to help your people take the creative path, not just once, but as a repeated pattern of behavior.

The third and most central idea we offer is about *how* to achieve that. In short, as a leader, you should not try to change the people you have; rather, you should change the environment they work in, so it becomes easier and more attractive to become an innovator. It is about *paving the way* for innovators, tweaking the workplace so potential innovators find it easier to take the creative path and become actual innovators. In this sense, we use the term "innovation architect" for the leader's role: one who designs, tweaks, and engineers the social and organizational space, building the daily architecture of innovation. This last point is of particular importance to leaders, and next, we explain the logic behind it.

Pave the Way: Building an Architecture of Innovation

In the early days of behavioral studies, the psychologist Kurt Lewin coined what has been called the most famous equation in the social sciences:

$$behavior = personality \times environment$$

Lewin's point was that in any given moment, our behavior can be understood as the result of the interaction between two things: who we are, and the situation we are in.

However, if you look at many of today's writings on leadership, you might think that personality was the only factor in the equation, because in the discussion of how to drive sustained behavior change in companies, many change makers tend to focus on changing the way people *think*. In an article from the *McKinsey Quarterly*, for instance, the authors summarize what the key to successful behavior change is (the emphasis is ours): "Success depends on *persuading* hundreds or thousands of groups and individuals to change the way they work, a transformation people will accept only if they can be *persuaded to think differently* about their jobs. In effect, CEOs must alter the mind-sets of their employees—no easy task."*

We call this approach the *mind-set approach*, and it characterizes much of the advice in the area of innovation. According to the mind-set approach, your job as a leader is first and foremost of a rhetorical nature: it is to persuade, to alter mind-sets, to change values, and to make people think differently. As a consequence, leaders have treated many innovation efforts as challenges of *communication*: of convincing, cajoling, storytelling, and explaining why innovation is necessary.

Beyond Mind-set Myopia

However, as Lewin's equation emphasizes, changing someone's mind is not the only way to change his or her behavior. If the people in your company suffer from a widespread lack of innovative behavior, you have to ask yourself: is that really a mind-set problem? Or is it perhaps a *systems* problem?

This point is pertinent because, if you consider the ways in which corporate leaders try to foster innovation in their people, you will notice that many put credence in the mind-set approach: they believe that the best way to change people's behavior is to change the people themselves, by changing their values, attitudes, mind-sets, and personal convictions. Leaders exhort their teams to think outside the box—whatever that means—implicitly suggesting that innovation is purely a

---

*Emily Lawson and Colin Price, "The Psychology of Change Management," *McKinsey Quarterly*, June 2003. In fairness, while the focus of the article is on mind-sets, the authors do acknowledge the power of structures and systems as well.

matter of mental effort. Managers hire motivational speakers to boost morale and reenergize their people, as if they were electrical toys in need of fresh batteries. Expansive values programs are initiated, training programs are run, and hordes of hapless employees are sent to change management courses to "let go of their fear of change." What all these approaches share is their failure to leverage the single most powerful source of influence on people's behavior: the organizational environment in which they work.

To be clear, the mind-set approach is not without merit. If well executed, the methods may sometimes generate useful results, at least in the short term. But the aim of an innovation architect is not just to generate a great new idea or two: it is to create *systemic* and *sustainable* innovation, to embed creativity in the DNA of the workplace. This is achieved only by altering more than just attitudes and mind-sets; self-discipline, motivational speeches, or training seminars alone cannot create sustainable change if the systems remain the same. The only way to *systematically* change behavior is, logically, by way of changing the systems.

"Keep an Open Mind" (and Other Useless Advice)

To understand why this is true—and why we need an architecture of innovation—consider the notion of "keeping an open mind" when confronting new ideas. This piece of advice is one of the most commonly shared insights in innovation courses; not a single manager hasn't heard of its importance. Only, how do you actually *do* that? Keeping an open mind is not that hard when you are sitting in a two-day offsite meeting and the professional facilitator has just told you to withhold judgment.

But what about the other 363 days of the year? What about when it is late Wednesday afternoon, you are stuck in the meeting from hell, the phone is buzzing, the budget report *still* isn't finished, you're late for that dinner with the in-laws, and the guy who took the last coffee didn't refill the pot, *again*. This is the kind of setting in which most people find themselves when they are suddenly ambushed by a new idea. In such situations, well-meaning exhortations about having an open mind or better listening skills are not very helpful. The problem is not that people don't understand the logic of listening. The problem is that at the moment when they need their listening skills, they are captives of a stronger, more powerful logic, namely, the one that resides in the architecture of their workplace.

Instead of relying on willpower and well-meaning advice to counter the systematic pressures of daily work, managers must create an *architecture* around the desired behavior: a collection of simple systems, routines, habits, and processes that can help them and their people with the job of receiving, storing, and filtering new ideas, all as an integrated and automatic part of their everyday work. In other words, managers should not try to create a perpetual state of open minds in their people; it's just not going to happen. Instead, they should assume and accept that, most of the time, people—including themselves—will have closed minds toward new ideas. Then, they should devise an architectural solution that can help overcome closed minds.

Fight Systems with Systems

The closed minds example conveys the core philosophy of the innovation architect; like a real architect, you affect people's behavior *indirectly*, through shaping their environment. Real architects work primarily with physical surroundings, with light and rooms and buildings. As an innovation architect, you work with something more comprehensive, namely, the sum of the physical, social, and professional environments that people work in. You work with what *Nudge* authors Richard Thaler and Cass Sunstein call the *choice architecture* of the workplace. The choice architecture, as we use the term here, is all the external, systemic factors that influence people's behavior at work: things like systems and structures, processes and places, strategies and policies, and even shared habits and routines.*

The architectural approach may require that you change the way you think about systems and creativity. Creative people in particular traditionally have strained relations with systems, structures, standards, and other perceived constraints on their creative freedom. Nowhere is this clearer than in big organizations where people often complain that "the systems" kill creativity, longingly thinking back to the halcyon days when the company was young and less bureaucratic.

Going back to the unstructured start-up days is not an option, however. Established companies require a different kind of innovation: they need a culture in which creativity is part of the corporate ecosystem. The key to building a creative culture is not to declare war on systems, processes, and policies, but to embrace and redesign them so they support and actively

---

*In the rest of this book, we consistently use the term *architecture* as shorthand for *choice architecture*. To avoid confusing it with *real* architecture, which is just one of the many systemic influences on people's behavior, we use alternative terms such as "office layout" to discuss the bricks-and-mortar kind.

enhance innovative behavior. Managers, in other words, have to *fight systems with systems*, creating an architecture of innovation in their teams and departments. The primary aim is to help people *behave* more like innovators. In the following sections, we cover exactly what that means, introducing the core model of the book.

The 5+1 Behaviors of Innovation as Usual

In their book *Influencer*, Kerry Patterson, Joseph Grenny, and their coauthors point out two important things about creating behavior change. First of all, if you are trying to instigate a new pattern of behavior, not all of the individual sub-behaviors that are involved are equally important: some behaviors are much more *vital* than others and must be the primary focus for change agents. Second, the authors point out, you must be very clear about what these vital behaviors *are* in order to make people adopt them.

For instance, as research into eating habits by Brian Wansink and others has shown, aiming to make people eat healthier food is a fine overall ambition, but it's way too abstract to be anything more than that. To have any hope of bringing about change, you have to get much more operational and hands on in defining the key behaviors you want people to adopt. One oft-cited example is the simple behavioral recommendation, "buy 1 percent milk," which has proven highly effective in the fight for better food habits. You can't expect people to change their behavior if you don't know what the new key behavior you want is.

The same logic applies to the pursuit of innovation as usual. The vision of "making people bring great ideas to life" really covers a whole lot of different behaviors, but not all of them are equally vital to the task. In this book, we have chosen to focus on what we call *the 5+1 keystone behaviors of innovation*, that is, the vital behavior patterns that you have to foster in your employees. The 5+1 behaviors also form the basic structure of this book, with a chapter dedicated to each behavior. In the rest of this chapter, we introduce the model and its elements in more detail, concluding with a description of the huge body of prior research in the innovation field on which we base our model. (The 5+1 keystone behaviors are outlined in the model in figure 1-1.)

FIGURE 1-1

The 5 + 1 keystone behaviors of innovation to promote in others

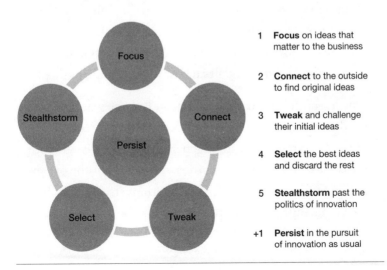

1 **Focus** on ideas that matter to the business

2 **Connect** to the outside to find original ideas

3 **Tweak** and challenge their initial ideas

4 **Select** the best ideas and discard the rest

5 **Stealthstorm** past the politics of innovation

+1 **Persist** in the pursuit of innovation as usual

Focus

We tend to associate innovation with people having the freedom to do whatever they want, but in the context of a regular job, that is often a bad idea. Employees who have complete freedom to innovate often pursue random ideas that don't matter to the business and might end up dividing their attention among various small side projects that don't go anywhere. Given the constraints of day-to-day pressure, innovators succeed when their leaders give them a clear and limiting *focus*, and when that focus is directed at something that can create value for the company. When pursuing innovation in a regular workplace, the cardinal rule is this: *focus beats freedom*. Innovation architects must *help their people focus their efforts on what matters*.

One leader who learned this firsthand was Mike Kendall, a senior executive we worked with over several years as he drove innovation within the European division of a large company—the name is confidential, so we'll call it NutroFoods.* Kendall headed a small team of leaders based in Switzerland, and during the team's first, systematic forays into fostering innovation in the various European country subsidiaries, the team didn't direct people's search for innovation. This experience taught the team a key lesson that one of Kendall's fellow managers shared with us:

> One lesson from our early efforts in Europe was that we need to connect the search for ideas to the strategic aims of the operation. Instead of generally saying "give us your ideas," we need to preselect the issues we want the organization to focus on. What is an important strategic problem we are facing? Let's ask people to look for solutions *there*.

*Due to confidentiality concerns, all identifying details of the NutroFoods examples in this book have been disguised.

The members of Kendall's team took this lesson to heart as they continued to push innovation in the local subsidiaries. In particular, Kendall started giving much more guidance on the *kind* of innovation that he wanted to see, directing his people to an underexplored but strategically important area:

> Our search for new ideas has typically focused on our products and the way they are delivered. But NutroFoods is not just in the business of shipping products—really, we are in the business of making people's lives better, which involves taking a much wider perspective on the customers and the many other stakeholders that are part of our world. In the subsidiaries, there was little focus on those aspects of our business; in effect, we were still thinking in terms of the model that characterized our business in the 1980s. So we asked people to focus explicitly on the bigger picture: can you go beyond the products? Can you think creatively about the other stakeholders in our world?

As Kendall and his team pushed this new focus area, NutroFoods's European subsidiaries started coming up with lots of new, impactful initiatives. In Germany, for instance, the local team worked with a third party to improve the *societal* benefits of their products, taking a wider perspective on the lives of their customers and strengthening NutroFoods's status as a trusted partner within the local business ecosystem. Success from this early initiative spurred a similar effort, first in Holland and later growing to include twenty-seven other countries in Europe and beyond.

As a result of this and several other innovative ideas, many targeting the new focus area Kendall and his team promoted, NutroFoods's European division managed to surpass its ambitious growth goals with a comfortable margin, demonstrating to the rest of the organization that the focused pursuit of daily innovation could create real results. Many members of Kendall's team gained high-profile leadership positions worldwide as NutroFoods's senior leadership took note of the results. As for Kendall himself, he was promoted to head up NutroFoods's commercial business globally; at the time of writing, he is working to spread the innovation virus to the rest of the organization, using the power of focus to drive results.

In chapter 2, we shall explain why innovation needs focus, why it tends to beat freedom, and how you, as a leader, can work to direct your people's pursuit of innovation.

Connect

A second, vital innovation behavior is that of *connecting* to new worlds. As a general rule, people won't get good ideas when they are isolated in their offices, or when their only sources of new input are the same newscasts and trade journals that everybody else in your industry follows. The cardinal rule here is, *insight comes from the outside*. Most ideas aren't in fact invented from scratch, but are instead examples of what University of California professor Andrew Hargadon calls *recombinant innovation*—that is, ideas that are pieced together by combining existing bits of knowledge in new ways. Innovation, in other words, is a bit like a puzzle whose pieces are distributed across the world. To expose people to these building blocks of innovation, leaders must *help their people connect to outside input*. Your current customers are one such rich source of knowledge, but they are not the only one; people can also find new ideas by connecting with colleagues from other departments or even with domains that are not related to your business.

The power of connecting people is now widely considered critical to innovation. Personally, we encountered our first memorable, if anecdotal, example of this many years ago at a major television broadcaster that had just instigated a no-smoking policy in its offices.* The broadcaster's various divisions normally had little contact, but because of the smoking ban, smokers from all manner of different departments were suddenly brought together daily, exchanging thoughts and ideas as they stood outside, puffing on their cigarettes. With the new policy, the company had inadvertently built a *creative space*, and according to the people we talked to, it led the broadcaster's people to come up with several good ideas. One such random interaction led to the development of a new technology that allowed television viewers to upload photos from their cellphones directly onto the screen so they could appear during live broadcasts, a technology that would eventually become a new source of revenue in the TV business.

Due to the open innovation movement that currently dominates the innovation industry, what the broadcaster did by accident has now become a deliberate and widespread practice. Countless stories abound of good ideas that have been spotted because companies helped their people connect to new worlds. Recently, some of the most prominent examples have arguably been Procter & Gamble's embrace of open innovation,

---

*We know this story from interviews we conducted with the broadcaster's employees many years ago, as part of a consulting assignment. We have chosen to call it an anecdote here as we didn't dig deeper in the story back then, but we have checked our current telling of the story with two former employees.

described in A.G. Lafley and Ram Charan's book *The Game-Changer*; innovation front-runner IDEO's widely emulated practices of having their people immerse themselves in new fields; and, of course, Apple's hugely successful habit of connecting and combining various external ideas and technologies to create breakthrough products, from the original Macintosh to the latest batch of i-devices. The next addition to the creativity canon is likely to be the iconic story shared in Walter Isaacson's biography of Steve Jobs: when Jobs designed the Pixar offices, he famously put the restrooms in the center of the building, creating a natural forcing function that made people interact with colleagues from other departments. Innovation architects must find ways to help their people connect to new worlds in similar ways. In chapter 3, we explain how you can do this.

Tweak

Ideas are not born perfect. Quite the contrary, *first ideas are flawed*, and usually, the better the ultimate innovation, the more it will have been modified between the first idea and the final implementation. The way to do this is through *tweaking*, i.e. a rapid-fire mix of testing and analysis.* Testing ideas quickly and repeatedly before they are ready—often called rapid prototyping—is an essential success strategy for innovators, and through the work of people such as Steve Blank and IDEO's Kelley brothers, it has become standard

---

*Our selection of the term *tweaking* is partly inspired by Malcolm Gladwell, who uses the term in a *New Yorker* article from 2011. The idea of tweaking is also related to the concept of *pivoting*, a word that is used in Silicon Valley to signify when start-ups nimbly (or not so nimbly) change their direction, based on learnings from their first forays into the market.

practice in the professional innovation community. But most people working in organizations will feel very uncomfortable with the notion of prototyping. For reasons both personal and professional, they often end up sitting in a dark corner for ages, polishing their idea to perfection before they put it out in the world. Innovation architects have to *help people test and challenge their ideas constantly*, exposing them to frequent feedback and promoting a culture of rapid learning and experimentation.

We personally saw the power of tweaking at work as we followed a regional manager, Heinrich Toledo.* Toledo worked for a large, diversified conglomerate, and some years ago, he was heading up its adhesives business in Central and Eastern Europe. Because Toledo worked with many different country managers in the region, he enforced a policy of rapid and constant experimentation.

For instance, the country managers knew that for new experiments, Toledo would approve pretty much anything under a certain limit, with no need for documentation. One manager described the approvals process: "I call Heinrich [Toledo] and say we are growing, I share the figures, and say we should try this new idea. We will need this much money to do it, and we will repay it in six months. He says, 'Go for it and give me the details later.'"

Toledo's willingness to let his country managers experiment with new ideas created a strong sense of loyalty among them. As one of them put it, "I have freedom to act. It is my business, it is my country. When the people from headquarters try to

*Not his real name. The case is from a series of engagements Miller did in 2004, working in Europe.

micromanage us, we feel like idiots. Do they think we work against the company? Toledo does not do this."

However, while Toledo allowed his managers to experiment, he also balanced this freedom with an extensive communication effort, both with him and between different managers. If one country manager tried something new, Toledo would soon call the other country managers and tell them about it. He also set up regular feedback sessions among the managers, explicitly having them challenge each other's ideas as vigorously as possible. Every three months, for instance, all the regional managers would spend three full days on a highly interactive offsite, helping each other solve problems, sharing best practices, and exploring new possibilities. Via this process, Toledo not only fostered cross-fertilization of ideas, but also ensured that the managers didn't pursue experiments that were *too* ill advised, effectively balancing their freedom with a certain level of sanity checking. And it worked. Through his system of encouraging constant experimentation and frequent feedback, Toledo delivered consistent annual growth rates of 15 percent to 20 percent, leading his region from 10 percent to 22.7 percent of the adhesives global sales in the span of two years. Similarly, by promoting a mix of responsible experimentation and frequent feedback sessions, innovation architects must help people tweak their ideas and work on bringing them to life rapidly.

Select

To the person who gets them, all ideas are divine in their perfection. But the dispassionate and somewhat unpleasant reality is that *most ideas are bad ideas*, and that makes it necessary for companies to master the discipline of filtering ideas, selecting which to invest in and which to discard.

This act of selecting ideas, though, comes with its own pitfalls. Research across a diverse set of disciplines has taught us that, when left to their own devices, people suffer from a hearty mix of cognitive and structural biases when they evaluate new ideas, making them prone to bad judgment calls. For this reason, it is necessary to optimize the decision environment of filtering, creating strong architectural support systems that can help the *gatekeepers* of your business make better judgment calls.

Mark Turrell, CEO of Orcasci and an expert in idea filtering, shared a thought-provoking example from his work within the business unit of a large US auto-parts manufacturer. To find new ways of generating cost savings, the business unit head Turrell worked with had run an internal idea contest, and as an experiment, he decided to divide the resulting ideas into two similar batches and then assign the job of evaluating them to not one, but two different groups of gatekeepers.

The experiment dramatically illustrated how gatekeepers can differ when left to their own devices. One group was able to complete its filtering work and recommend how to implement the top ideas within ten man-hours, getting the work done in two meetings. The second group took more than one hundred man-hours to evaluate the ideas and had not yet completed the filtering process. Remarkably, as the business unit head eventually looked into the results of the two selection processes, he found that the quality of their recommendations seemed largely similar. Intrigued by the difference, he asked one of his people to study the two groups and figure out what had happened.

As it turned out, the primary difference was the two groups' leadership. The ten-hour group was led by a manager who was extremely goal oriented and trained in project management. Under his leadership, the group had first speed-filtered the list, rapidly discarding everything but the top twenty-five ideas. Then they had discussed these in depth, creating a short list of twenty ideas. They eventually force-ranked them into a final list with only ten recommendations. The leader of the other group, in comparison, wanted to achieve consensus and personally believed that all ideas deserved the same level of analysis, even if it was just to show respect to the efforts of the idea submitters. Thus, he asked his group to investigate each idea, including follow-up interviews, desk research, and frequent group meetings to share insights from the analysis.

From this experiment, the head of the business unit realized it was necessary to approach the idea gatekeeping process more systematically, making it a core competence in his business. However, he also felt that using only the most efficient approach would likely fail to spot long-term opportunities. Eventually, he ended up creating two different gatekeeping processes: a primary one that was fast and aimed at quick wins, and a secondary one that was more meticulous, aimed at exploring less obvious ideas that might have hidden potential. The business also started using a simple personality test, so the two review boards would be peopled with individuals who fit the respective purposes. It also implemented a short training program for gatekeepers. As a result, the business unit dramatically shortened the time to turn quick-win ideas into results, while also protecting the more vulnerable long-term ideas against overly efficient gatekeepers.

The need to consider the idea-filtering process is not relevant only to senior executives. In chapter 5, on *selecting*, we share a number of tips that managers at all levels can use to improve their gatekeeping practices. Innovation architects must *engineer the decision environment of the people who evaluate ideas.*

Stealthstorm

When working in an organization, there is no avoiding the reality of corporate politics; like it or not, *stealthstorming rules.** A remarkably large chunk of an innovator's time is spent dealing with various stakeholders, employing a mix of charm and organizational savvy to make ideas happen. But for various reasons, many innovators don't like to play politics, if they don't just ignore it completely, assuming that a good idea will sell itself. That assumption is dangerous to make; many great projects have been killed by organizational forces. Innovation architects must *help create the political space for innovation*, paving the way for people to succeed.

In doing this, it is key to understand that politics, like power, is not just a negative force. When used right, it can propel things

---

*We define stealthstorming as follows; stealthstorm (verb): *to pursue innovation in a manner that is compatible with the existing cultural and political realities of the organization.* Stealthstorming thus implies a strong political awareness of the corporate culture (which is seen as a given, in the short term at least) and contrasts with more revolutionary, flamboyant or overtly counter-cultural approaches to innovation. We discuss the concept and its meaning in more detail in chapter 6.

forward and move new ideas safely past obstacles. We saw this powerful dynamic at work in the launch of pfizerWorks, a successful innovation initiative that Jordan Cohen, an HR manager working in Pfizer's global headquarters in New York, created from scratch.

The basic idea behind pfizerWorks was simple: it aimed at eradicating grunt work. Cohen had noticed that many of Pfizer's well-paid, highly educated people were in fact spending a lot of their time doing tasks that were wasting their time, such as vetting spreadsheets, tweaking PowerPoints, gathering data, or doing basic-level Internet research. By connecting them with pre-vetted teams of virtual assistants working in and outside the United States, pfizerWorks effectively enabled Pfizer's employees to outsource the boring parts of their jobs, allowing them to focus on more high-impact work and making them vastly more productive, both personally and to Pfizer.

The initial tests of the service were promising, and many of the first users Cohen asked to test it became regular users. However, Cohen had effectively built the first prototype working under the radar, and the idea didn't have any kind of official support, much less a proper home or a budget—things that were becoming increasingly necessary as the project grew in scope. To move past the experimental stage and have proper impact on the then eighty-thousand-employee organization, Cohen faced the task of securing support for the project.

This is where David Kreutter, a senior commercial manager and one of Cohen's informal mentors, stepped into the picture. For some time, Kreutter had followed the project with interest, and when Cohen needed to demonstrate the value of pfizerWorks, Kreutter used his influence to find a creative workaround:

> We had some companies we wanted to do a general business profile summary on, as potential partnership candidates. The idea was to use pfizerWorks to do this, instead of having the investment banks do it, as was customary— only, that recommendation was not endorsed by the project leaders at Pfizer, who preferred to leave the task to the investment banks, despite their much higher cost. But since pfizerWorks was so cheap to use, I decided to try it anyway, authorizing that we ran the two searches in parallel. As a result, we could compare pfizerWorks' output to those of the selected investment banks—and by doing that, we obtained our first piece of evidence that pfizerWorks could deliver the same quality as these famed investment banks, for a fraction of the cost.

This was one of many instances where Kreutter helped Cohen deal with the organizational barriers, gradually paving the way for pfizerWorks to survive and succeed. Kreutter also provided essential advice along the way, guiding Cohen on how to position the initiative internally, helping him secure a meeting with Pfizer's vice chairman, and finding an organizational home for the initiative. As a result, as the project gained more and more users, it eventually became recognized as a success story, and Cohen ended up being featured in *Business Week*, *Fast Company*, and several other business publications.

There is little doubt that the main credit for pfizerWorks belongs to Cohen; without his personal abilities to define a vision, build a committed team, and lead the project through the implementation phase, the idea would not have happened. Yet Cohen is the first to point out that without the support and air cover that Kreutter provided, pfizerWorks would likely have taken far longer to create. In a similar vein, innovation architects must help their people navigate the politics of innovation, aiding them in engaging in the fifth keystone behavior, stealthstorming.

Persist

Any leader, via her personal presence, can make people engage in the five keystone behaviors once or twice. But the ultimate challenge is to make people *persist* in those behaviors, making the behaviors an ingrained part of what people do, even on the days when you are not there to guide and direct their efforts. Ultimately, systems and structures are not enough on their own: a final piece of the innovation puzzle is to leverage the power of *personal motivation*, combining individual interests and reward systems in a way that makes people more likely to keep going in the face of adversity. The cardinal rule here is, *creativity is a choice*. Innovation architects must find ways to help their people *continue to exhibit* the five key behaviors, tweaking the pursuit of innovation so it is more likely to foster perseverance.

Perhaps the most potent example occurred in NutroFoods Belgium, a sixty-person sales and marketing subsidiary that was part of the European innovation initiative we described earlier. As Kendall started driving innovation in Europe, NutroFoods Belgium had recently gotten a new country manager, the forty-year-old Marc Granger.

From the start, Granger clearly had his hands full. The Belgian subsidiary had previously done well, but as he took over, the small business was fighting wars on several fronts.

Growth had declined. Employee satisfaction was at an all-time low, with internal surveys reporting that only 39 percent of his people enjoyed working at NutroFoods. Employee turnover, at 30 percent, was double the industry average in Belgium, and sick leaves were high, creating a significant strain on the small outfit. In diagnosing the lack of innovation, Granger said:

> It was clear to me from the start that our people didn't lack creative abilities; many of them had already shown they were capable of delivering great results. Rather, I felt that the barriers to innovation revolved around the issue of motivation. It was a very "manager-only" driven company, where people felt they needed to get a manager's approval before doing anything not directly ordered, and there was a clear bias towards trying to "do it all" instead of prioritizing and saying no to things. People did not feel any strong sense of ownership of their work; it was top-down all the way, which prevented people from coming up with new ideas. That is what I wanted to change.

Granger's way to do that was remarkable: using an upcoming office move as a turning point, he decided to change the entire culture of the company, giving people much more freedom to decide what they would work on. Employees, not management, decided the layout of the new office. Many people wanted to abolish the rigid nine-to-five regimen, so Granger decided to allow people to determine their own working hours, as long as they delivered on the results. And most importantly, as Granger asked them to help make innovation happen, he made it clear that the projects would not be chosen by the management team. While everybody had to pick *something* to work on, each employee was entirely free to work on whatever project he or she found most relevant. Granger's only requirement was that the chosen project supported the overall aim of making NutroFoods Belgium a better and more innovative place to work. By doing this, Granger managed to tap into one of the most potent sources of persistence: people's personal interests and priorities. The results were remarkable. Through a river of minor improvements and small but impactful ideas, NutroFoods achieved a lasting turnaround:

- Employee turnover was halved in one year. By 2011, it had fallen to 9 percent.

- Employee satisfaction doubled within a year of the move, going from 39 percent to 74 percent.

- Growth rebounded with a vengeance; one year after the move, NutroFoods Belgium became one of the most profitable subsidiaries in Europe. By 2011, revenues had grown almost 70 percent compared to when Granger started.

- Several other subsidiaries in Northern Europe were inspired to take a similar approach, with equally strong results.

- Granger himself was promoted; he is now leading five thousand people in Asia, where he continues to drive growth through his work as an innovation architect.

Significantly, NutroFoods Belgium also received another external validation of its work. At the start of the innovation journey, Granger had signed the company up for a Belgian business magazine's "Best Place to Work" survey. On the day of the move to a new building, we listened to the management team members as they made a public commitment to their people that within four years, NutroFoods Belgium would win that survey and become Belgium's best place to work.

After a one-year delay, that's exactly what NutroFoods Belgium did. After five years of steadily climbing ratings, Belgian newspapers announced that NutroFoods Belgium had become number one in the survey, marking the culmination— but not the end—of a spectacular innovation journey.* All things considered, that's not bad for a small group of managers with no budget for innovation.

In the final chapter of the book, on persistence, we share some tips on how you can engender the same level of commitment and perseverance in your people, making them take the creative path in their daily work.

Why These Behaviors?

Countless academic papers have been published on the topics of creativity and innovation, and many have offered models for innovative behavior. The 5+1 framework we present here stems from a mix of existing models and past research, filtered through the lens of our extensive personal experience working with and alongside managers. As such, it is born purely of practical concerns; it should not be considered a comprehensive theoretical model, but is intended as a tactical, hands-on guide

---

*The Great Place to Work survey is done by an independent institute. In the year NutroFoods Belgium won it, the award was given in four categories, namely small, medium-sized, and large companies, with a separate category for governmental organizations. NutroFoods won the number-one placement in the category for companies with 50 to 500 employees.

to the most essential aspects of innovation. As we show in the coming chapters, our choice of the 5+1 behaviors is supported by a mix of case studies and qualitative and quantitative data, but ultimately, our core deciding criterion for inclusion has been a simpler one: in our experience, *where do most would-be innovators tend to go wrong?*

In addition, the relative simplicity of the model is a point in itself. Innovation is a complex phenomenon, and given half a minute, any student of creativity will be able to add several other behaviors to the mix. However, experience has taught us that doing so is counterproductive. When you work with people who also have to juggle many responsibilities other than innovation, the models you use have to pass the simplicity test: a model is only useful to the extent people can remember it unaided. As one senior manager told us after his people had gone through an in-depth course on creative methods, delivered by a well-known innovation consultancy: "I think the methods are good, but I also think the set of twenty tools we learned is overwhelming; after all, we don't need to become innovation ninjas. Instead, let's pick three or four of the most useful tools, like reframing the problem, and focus on getting those key things right."

In that spirit, we have chosen to focus on the 5+1 behaviors. Notably, the need to focus also applies to leaders: as you start improving your people's ability to bring great ideas to life, you should not necessarily try to make your people excel at each behavior. Unless you work in an absolute pit of noninnovation, chances are that they are already doing *some* things right; only part of the system is blocking progress. We strongly recommend that you start using the 5+1 framework as a diagnostic tool, scanning your business and identifying the biggest behavioral bottlenecks to innovation and then focusing on fixing them.

Think of the innovation process as a garden hose that has become entangled: once you find and straighten the spot where the hose is twisted, the water can start flowing freely. (See also the box, "The Innovation Ecosystem: Beyond Step-by-Step Models.")

The Innovation Ecosystem: Beyond Step-by-Step Models

How and when do the five keystone behaviors occur? In the history of creativity research, the earliest models of the process tended to portray innovation as something that can be divided into separate, step-by-step phases or stages; Graham Wallas's 1926 model, for instance, went from "preparation" through "incubation" to "illumination" and "verification."* However, it has become clear that this sequential "First do A, then move on to B" perspective is *not* a very good model for what really happens during an innovation process. Rather, the behaviors take place repeatedly throughout the entire process, as innovators continually rotate back and forth between the different "lenses" of focusing, connecting, tweaking, selecting, and stealthstorming. Hence, as an innovation architect, the challenge is to create an *ecosystem* at work in which the five behaviors can occur on an ongoing and iterated basis, supporting each other.

*Wallas's model is still in use in some parts of the innovation community; we have seen several advertising agencies that subscribe to it, in theory at least. The model is described in Graham Wallas, "The Art of Thought" (San Diego, CA: Harcourt, Brace and Company, 1926).

On the Shoulders of Several Giants

Although we are academics at heart, you won't find our names in prestigious scientific research journals. Both of us get our energy from being close to the action, and we have jointly spent more than four decades working in companies, acting as coaches, caddies, students, instructors, and occasionally long-term therapists for the managers we worked with. We like to say that we live on the first floor of the ivory tower: close enough to the ground to see the nitty-gritty of daily management, but still high enough to gain a bit of perspective on the whole thing. Yet, we could never have written this book, much less been of any help to managers, had it not been for the tremendous amount of work that countless others have invested in understanding innovation.

The advice we share in this book stands on the shoulders of giants past and present, hailing from many different fields. First, our book builds on knowledge derived from the dual fields of innovation and creativity research. Since the 1950s, more than fifteen thousand academic papers have been published on the topic of creativity alone, and we owe our current body of knowledge to the countless number of academics and scholars, past and present, who have dedicated their careers to the painstaking exploration of innovation's white spaces. Overall, besides the sources that we mention throughout individual chapters, the advice we share owes a particular debt to the ideas of Clayton Christensen; Teresa Amabile; Michael Tushman; Vijay Govindarajan and Chris Trimble; Gary Hamel; Mihaly Csikszentmihalyi and Jacob Getzels; Andrew Hargadon; Robert G. Cooper; Michael Mumford; Robert I. Sutton;

Robert Sternberg; and R. Keith Sawyer and Dean Keith Simonton; as well as the recent, practical work of companies such as IDEO, Innosight, Prehype, and Vivaldi Partners.

In addition to the innovation field, two other domains have been prominent in shaping our thinking. The closely related field of entrepreneurship studies has yielded critical insights into the realities of forming new ventures; Steve Blank is a central figure, as is Saras Sarasvathy and her research on effectuation. Second, the burgeoning and ever-evolving field of behavioral studies has been critical to the development of this book. Within this field, we owe thanks to a hearty mix of academics, practitioners, and world-class conveyors of knowledge: Daniel Kahneman and Amos Tversky's mapping of decision biases; Chip Heath and Dan Heath's work on behavior change; Brian Wansink's studies of eating habits; Paco Underhill's studies of shopping behavior; Andy Clark and David Chalmers' extended mind concept; Philip Zimbardo's work on the power of systems; and many others. A special recognition is due to Richard Thaler and Cass Sunstein, whose clearly expressed ideas about nudges and choice architecture helped shape and sharpen our own more nascent ideas about the architecture of innovation. At the end of the book, we have included an appendix of further reading, listing a range of authors and thought leaders who have provided both the foundation and much of the ammunition for this book.

To this immense work, we add our personal perspective on innovation, trying to elicit what we believe are the most essential, unmissable lessons that are relevant for managers working in regular businesses. Our work as academics, teachers, consultants, and occasional entrepreneurs has shaped that perspective.

Through our work with IESE Business School in particular, we have met with senior executives as they talked about creating new growth; with midlevel managers as they struggled to turn the search for innovation into specific initiatives; and with low-level employees as they reacted to those innovation initiatives, sometimes in very different ways from what their leaders had hoped for. In some cases, we followed innovation initiatives over several years and saw what happened *after* the honeymoon phase, when the managers who instigated the initiatives moved on to greener pastures. We followed companies in the United States, Europe, Latin America, Asia, and Africa; we studied companies in a broad range of industries, covering airlines, banks, web start-ups, broadcasting, pharmaceuticals, fashion, luxury goods, petrochemicals, telecoms, consumer goods, electronics, retailers, medical devices, sports apparel, auto manufacturing, and major conglomerates. We also have some hands-on experience with innovation. Wedell-Wedellsborg is involved in the entrepreneurial scene in New York and has personally founded two start-ups in the digital space (both of which are still around). We now delve into the sum of all this, starting with the first keystone behavior: that of making your people *focus* in their pursuit of innovation.

CHAPTER 2

FOCUS

HOW TO MAKE PEOPLE FOCUS ON IDEAS THAT MATTER

FOCUS BEATS FREEDOM
Leaders must limit and direct the
search for innovation

Most people associate innovation with the idea of *freedom*: giving your employees the space and the opportunity to pursue new ideas, free of all constraints. But, in fact, if you are to make innovation happen as part of a daily work environment, you will almost always generate better results if you actively *direct and limit* people's search for innovation, making sure they concentrate their creative efforts on something that matters to the business. By providing this guidance, innovation architects create the first keystone behavior: *focus*.

How Focus Saved Lonza's Thiamin Business

Consider the story of how Felix Previdoli, a leader we know from the Swiss company Lonza, discovered the power of focus. Lonza, a major supplier to the life sciences industry, has twenty-eight facilities in Europe, the United States, and Asia. In 2011, its eight thousand three hundred employees achieved sales of close to $3 billion. Lonza's leaders had long recognized the creative potential of their employees, and across the company, managers used various ways of collecting ideas from their people, ranging from suggestion boxes to online forms to the occasional workshop sessions. Like many other companies, following the philosophy that "there's no such thing as a bad idea," Lonza generally didn't try to direct or limit its people's creativity, but openly listened to whatever suggestions came up. It carefully catalogued and stored every single incoming proposal, big or small, promising or mundane, in various databases of ideas across the company.

The Problem: Too Many Random Ideas

This had been the state of affairs for some years when Previdoli, a longtime Lonza employee with a PhD in chemical engineering, entered the scene. Previdoli had been promoted to head of R&D and new business development for one of the divisions. He made it his job to study Lonza's idea pipeline, stepping into the role of an innovation architect. He quickly realized that something wasn't working. The ideas of the employees were collected, all right, but then very little happened to them. Previdoli commented: "When I reviewed Lonza's idea database, there were several hundred ideas in it—everything from new product ideas to small process improvements or suggestions for automating some minor procedure. Only, most of those ideas had been sitting there for years, with very little follow-up. It was a bit of a black hole for ideas, and I think our people had started to notice."

As Previdoli investigated the reasons, he found that part of the problem was managerial: nobody had created a process for what would happen to the ideas *after* they were collected. How would they be evaluated? Who had the expertise to do it? How would the company find the resources to proceed with the best ideas? To fix this, Previdoli started the gradual work of creating an architecture that would support the entire process from idea to implementation.

But, interestingly, Previdoli realized that it wasn't just a capacity problem. The problem was also that the company received *too many random ideas*. Somehow, the "everything goes" philosophy produced a torrent of mostly decent but not great ideas, most of which would not make a big difference to Lonza. So Previdoli decided to try a different tack: instead of asking people for whatever ideas they could come up with, he would try to focus their hunt for ideas, setting very specific limits for the kinds of ideas he wanted to see.

"I Only Want Ideas That . . ."

The opportunity soon came along, as one of Lonza's products—the name is confidential, so we'll call it "Thiamin"—came under heavy price pressure. Lonza had manufactured and sold Thiamin for decades, making good profits on it, but now, foreign competitors with lower labor costs had started to price Lonza out of the market. As a consequence, Previdoli's division would have to close down its Thiamin plants, unless, that is, it could find a way to drastically lower the costs. So together with Lonza's division heads, Previdoli sent out a highly focused call for ideas to the company's personnel, explaining that they *only* wanted ideas that:

- Would focus on improving the Thiamin manufacturing process and

- Would deliver at least 30 percent cost savings

The highly focused brief paid off immediately. Given a clear direction and tangible objectives to achieve, Lonza's people sank their creative teeth into the challenge. In the space of a few weeks, Previdoli and his team had received four different viable ideas for how to lower costs. They tested the ideas at once and implemented the most promising one in a trial plant. It performed far beyond expectations: through a drastic simplification of the process, Lonza increased the productivity by a factor of 100 and reduced the manufacturing asset cost of Thiamin by 75 percent. Lonza's operation was saved, and shareholders were delighted as the company realized millions of dollars in cost savings.

The Hidden Cost of "Freedom to Innovate"

The Thiamin story is an example of the tremendous power of focus. It shows the difference when leaders act as innovation architects, directing the search for innovation and setting clear and limiting goalposts up for their people. Perhaps more interestingly, the story is also a testament to the surprising weakness of giving people freedom to innovate. Because when you think about it, the most remarkable part of the story is the question, why wasn't the idea spotted *earlier*? Why hadn't Lonza's army of scientists and engineers seen the opportunity? Thiamin wasn't a new product. In fact, when Previdoli came on the scene, Lonza had already been producing Thiamin for over two decades, using the old, expensive process. In other words, for *more than twenty years*, Lonza's philosophy of giving people freedom to innovate failed to identify an opportunity that could have created significant cost savings, directly feeding top-line earnings. The discovery didn't hinge on some new process that had only just become known. In all that time, there was literally nothing that prevented the researchers at Lonza from identifying the opportunity. Nothing, that is, except the lack of a leader with a clear strategy for what he wanted his people to achieve—and the understanding that when it comes to innovation, focus often beats freedom.

Failure to Focus: A Widespread Barrier

The idea that innovation benefits from direction is not new. Since the psychologist J. P. Guilford unofficially launched the field of creativity studies in a famous 1950 lecture, research into creative processes has repeatedly established that you often get better and more original ideas if you put some kind of constraints or limitations on people's ideas, instead of giving them complete freedom. Within the more narrow confines of business creativity as well, innovation scholars like Harvard's Teresa Amabile have painstakingly gathered empirical evidence that setting clear goals for innovation efforts tends to make for much better outcomes. But to what extent is this insight actually applied in real life?

Both our personal experience and some of the available data suggest that the answer is "not a lot." According to a study we conducted in 2011 with Capgemini's Koen Klokgieters and Freek Duppen, the failure to direct people's search for new ideas may be the most widespread barrier to innovation.

In the study, we zoomed in on one specific expression of focus, namely, the concept of an innovation strategy. We surveyed 260 executives worldwide, most of whom held formal innovation roles, that is, they had titles such as chief innovation officer, director of innovation, and similar titles, indicating that their companies were not oblivious to the importance of innovating. Yet, our data revealed that only 42 percent of the companies we surveyed had an explicit innovation strategy. Furthermore, when we asked what most constrained their company's ability to innovate, the single most frequent reply was "the absence of a well-articulated innovation strategy." (See the box, "Survey: What Do Innovation Strategies Contain?")

Survey: What Do Innovation Strategies Contain?

At the top level of corporate guidance, many companies (or their chief innovation officers) have adopted the practice of crafting an innovation strategy. However, this practice is, if not nascent, then still in its adolescence. There is currently no unified framework or an agreed-upon definition of what an innovation strategy is.*

For this reason, we asked the respondents in our survey to specify what their innovation strategy contained. In the

---

*In fact, through prior surveys, the people we worked with at Capgemini found that even innovation experts often have trouble explaining what an innovation strategy is.

list of results, notice in particular that less than half set specific targets for innovation, only four in ten define which partners to collaborate with, and one in five does not clarify how innovation is aligned with the corporate strategy. In the following findings, the number in parentheses is the percentage of respondents who included the item in their innovation strategy:

- **Alignment with Corporate Strategy (80%).** How will the pursuit of innovation help create value for the business?

- **Technology (64%).** Which technologies are we focused on?

- **Markets (62%).** Which markets do we seek to innovate in? Which customer segments?

- **Innovation Culture (58%).** What kind of internal culture will we seek to create?

- **Innovation Processes (55%).** Which systems and structures will help us innovate?

- **Internal Capabilities (47%).** Which innovation skills and capabilities will we develop in our people?

- **Targets (44%).** What specific targets will we achieve through innovation?

- **Partners (40%).** Which external parties will we seek to collaborate with, and how?

Surveys that went beyond innovation specialists to a wider group of employees and managers also confirmed the finding. In a global survey of 1,356 managers, for instance, researchers Jay Jamrog, Mark Vickers, and Donna Bear found that the second and third most cited barriers to innovation were, respectively, "no formal strategy for innovation" and "lack of clear goals/priorities."

Goals, priorities, and strategies for innovation are, of course, three different things, but what they share is this: they give employees an answer to the question, "What should I focus on?" In that perspective, it is clear that beyond the exhortation to think outside the box, many managers fail to tell their employees where they are supposed to go and what they are supposed to achieve.

Lost in the Woods: What Is the Problem with Freedom?

To understand *why* focus can create better results than freedom, it is necessary to zoom in on the daily realities that your employees face, looking at the micro-level of their everyday behaviors. As a thought experiment, put yourself in their shoes. During an average workday, employees make hundreds of small decisions about what to do next, some of them deliberate, most of them automatic. Taking the road of business as usual is relatively easy to do. But what if your boss has just asked you to innovate, without any further guidance on what that means? The reality is that as an employee, once you look away from the main road and think about heading into unexplored territory, you will quickly come face to face with a whole lot of *choices*. For instance: What direction should we head in? Are there any no-go areas? Can I explore ideas that are not directly related to our business? What kind of result counts as a good outcome? Should I look for internal stuff, think about new products, aim for cost savings, rethink our marketing plans, fix small issues, shoot for the moon, or something else again? For that matter, when is the right time to start—today, tomorrow, next month?

Potential innovators face a vast and often bewildering array of decisions, and that generates at least three kinds of trouble. First, research into decision making has found what author Barry Schwartz calls *the paradox of choice*, namely, that having lots of options can exert a paralyzing effect on decision makers. Simply put, if people don't know where to start or what to aim for, chances are they won't start at all, but will instead turn their attention to something more tangible, such as doing business as usual. Second, the lack of direction also means that people may pursue wildly different goals, making it harder to succeed. Third, a more subtle danger awaits: that people do as you ask and go boldly innovating—only they do so in an area that has absolutely no value to your business.

Collect Ideas That Are Worth Implementing

For an example of how the "innovation needs freedom" philosophy can take a business down the wrong path, consider how many companies run internal *idea contests*. When novice innovation leaders attempt to leverage the creativity of their employees, often they will simply call for ideas and then hope for the best, praying that whatever comes crawling out of their company's collective subconsciousness will not be too toe-curlingly awful to implement. Often it *is* awful, though, because as creativity researchers have found, absent a specific, focused problem statement, people don't tend to come up with very original or interesting ideas. In such situations, a novel idea may arise, but it will be awash in a torrent of barely disguised complaints ("increase our salary please"), mundane suggestions ("more vegetarian options in the cafeteria"), wistful thinking ("let's stop having meetings"), unfiltered blue-sky rubbish ("let our customers decide how much they want to pay for our products"), and the occasional, *truly* deranged idea ("reduce executive pay levels").* Managers then proceed to implement a few "quick win" suggestions, but most ideas never go any further, perhaps because they are too difficult to evaluate, or because there is no real corporate motivation to take the ideas further. Of course, in a delicious irony few appreciate, the company may still judge the idea contest a great success, based on the core evidence that a great number of ideas were

---

*A quick remark, lest we incur the wrath of foodies everywhere. People often come up with relatively mundane ideas about improving the food selection, getting better parking conditions, and similar issues. Such ideas can be well worth implementing, not least if one of your key objectives is to increase employee satisfaction. But don't be mistaken: by and large, the ideas are about creature comforts, not about corporate performance. Despite decades of research, it is still not clear whether increasing employee happiness causes better performance; in fact, the link partially seems to go the *other* way, with people reporting increased workplace satisfaction, the better their company is doing. Again, that doesn't mean it's not worth doing; just don't expect the stock price to soar in tandem with the combinatorial possibilities at the salad bar.

produced by the initiative ("Our recent InnovationJam resulted in more than 350 ideas! Congratulations!").

The quick-win philosophy is not a bad one; by swiftly implementing small ideas, managers can show people that their ideas are taken seriously. But in an important sense, this approach misses a fundamental point. What Lonza's story really highlights is a shift in perspective. It's not about implementing the ideas you collect; it is about *making sure that the ideas you collect are worth implementing*. By clarifying the strategic purpose of innovation and then sharing it with people, innovation architects can make sure that people make the most of their search for innovation. This is why leaders must imbue their people's pursuit of innovation with some kind of direction. Depending on the specifics, the best vehicle for giving those directions will differ, as will the degree of autonomy it gives the employees; it may be a broad strategic statement for an entire company, or it may be a very specific goal, target, or end state that members of a team should try to achieve. But in essence, by giving advance thought to those issues and by sharing them in a way that makes them operational, leaders provide a *decision architecture* for their people: an external guiding (or forcing) function that helps them make good choices about where to invest their efforts. (See the box, "When Is Freedom Appropriate?")

Three Ways to Help People Focus

In the remainder of this chapter, we discuss how you can help people focus their search for innovation. Depending on your situation, you may want to think of this in various terms: as an

When Is Freedom Appropriate?

Freedom isn't all bad. Giving people complete freedom increases the chances that they will find a *really* unusual idea, coming from a completely unexpected angle. But giving people freedom also drastically increases the likelihood that they will spend their energy on *bad* ideas that won't create (timely) value for the company. (Remember, *most ideas are bad ideas.*) This trade-off, in our experience, does not work well for regular leaders, where the time horizon for delivering innovation results tends to be short. It can be more appropriate in R&D departments and similar places where there is more leeway for high-risk, high-reward projects.

In addition, freedom can be useful when dealing with a new, poorly understood domain. With emerging technologies, for instance, leaders may not be the best people to determine where the potential value is biggest. In such situations, giving people on the ground more freedom to determine or influence the focus can make sense.

Finally, focus should not be confused with putting all your bets in a single area. By having different focus areas for different groups, leaders can create a small portfolio of bets, spreading the risk and increasing the likelihood of success. Giving people freedom to determine their own focus is one way of doing this; another is to make sure there is a good spread in your various initiatives, mixing low-risk and high-risk projects and targeting different aspects of the business or the consumer landscape. (To read more on this, look at the literature on "innovation portfolios.")

innovation strategy, as a game plan, or simply as a goal statement like the one Previdoli gave his people at Lonza. What matters, in our experience, is not what you call it, but whether it helps people make good decisions. This entails getting three things right:

1. Clarify the objective: what are we trying to achieve?

2. Define the sandbox: what are the limits of the search?

3. Shift the search space: which *new* areas should people look at?

1. Clarify the Objective: What Are We Trying to Achieve?

Perhaps the most essential question is, what kind of *outcome* do you want people to strive for? In our definition of innovation— creating results by doing new things—you have to make sure people know what counts as a good result. By putting yourself in the shoes of an innovator, you can ask if there is a specific kind of outcome that would be particularly valuable to the business. If I have an idea for increasing employee satisfaction or reducing our carbon footprint, is that worth pursuing, or should I only consider projects that cut costs, increase market share, or something else? And what kind of outcome would make an idea attractive? Is a potential cost savings of 3 percent worth getting excited about, or do I need to aim higher to make it worth pursuing?

In the case of Lonza, Previdoli gave a very clear brief: his people needed to find ways to get 30 percent cost savings, because that was the level needed to save the Thiamin operation from competitive pressure. In NutroFoods Belgium, the management team also set a clear objective, namely, turning

NutroFoods into the country's best place to work within four years. Besides being a worthy goal in itself, this objective was crucial in driving down employee turnover (a key cost factor) and making the business succeed.

The answer, in your case, will depend on the situation, and you need to think in depth about the strategic situation before you can settle on the right objective. The following (nonexhaustive) list of possible innovation objectives can spur your thinking:

- Reach monthly sales target
- Increase market share in major markets
- Cut costs to improve competitiveness
- Increase retention of existing customers
- Reduce turnover of key employees
- Improve employer branding to attract better talent
- Decrease time-to-market for new products
- Circumvent regulatory obstacles in a foreign market
- Reduce dependency on a specific supplier
- Look innovative, to prepare for a sale of the business
- Simplify internal processes to improve flexibility
- Discover new or adjacent markets to enter
- Build customer awareness of a key issue
- Handle a public relations crisis
- Improve quality in manufacturing
- Make our products safer to use
- Exploit an existing, underutilized asset
- Defend our core market against a new entrant

Agreeing on the right objective can be more challenging than it seems once you bring other people into the discussion. A week before finishing this chapter, we spent several days in Kiev, working with a group of Russian managers on how to promote innovation within their one-thousand-person organization. The Russians were very strong on execution and gave us an elaborate and well-thought-out plan for what they would do over the next four months. But once we asked them to define the bigger objective—where should all of this lead, and how would that help the business?—all hell broke loose. As it turned out, the four managers had very different ideas about which aims mattered most to the business. Only through a hard, but important discussion did they start the process of getting aligned. Without a clear and shared notion of the desired *outcome*—first at the leadership level, and then among the employees—chances are that innovation efforts won't have much impact. As an innovation architect, you have to be clear on the objectives of innovating and communicate them widely.

At What Level Should Companies Decide the Focus?

Focus needs to happen at some level, but it does not have to happen at *all* levels. In one company we worked with, the regional leadership team members deliberately chose to let the individual country managers decide where to focus their people's efforts. The only hard guidelines they gave were the time line—when they had to deliver results on innovation—and the expected level of results. Beyond that, instead of giving a narrow focus, they made sure that their country managers all understood what the objectives of the business were and how the strategic landscape was changing. Having done this, they enabled their country managers to make good decisions about what to focus on in their own markets, giving them freedom to adapt to the local conditions while making sure that their choices would still be in line with the overall priorities of the business.

There are no hard and fast rules for where focus should occur. In markets with high degree of uncertainty, or with large local differences, delegating the decision of where to focus to the lower levels can make sense. In situations where there are great advantages from collaboration and synergy, or exceedingly clear and global strategic priorities, it can make sense to determine the scope higher in the organization.

2. Define the Sandbox:
What Are the Limits of the Search?

Along with a clear objective, people need some *constraints* on their search. If you think of innovation as a new path through the woods, then the objective tells people roughly where you'd like them to end up, while constraints tell them *how to get there*: which routes to take, which pitfalls to avoid, and perhaps what kind of travel companions to ask for advice.

We do not define a specific framework here, in part because we don't believe it is possible to define a one-size-fits-all framework that works across all levels and in all situations. Instead, to keep things practical, we present a list of typical questions that prospective innovators face. The list helps you consider whether your people can answer them clearly. For each question, ask yourself, is there a right (or wrong) answer, from the perspective of the business? If so, do your people know what that answer is?

- What is the right time horizon? How quickly do I need to deliver results? For instance, is it OK to pursue an idea that won't create results for the first two-and-a-half years? Is it OK to pursue something when the time horizon is uncertain?

- Which stakeholders should I focus on? Should I look at our existing customers only, or is it OK to explore ideas targeted at nonconsumers? What about ideas that target internal people or partners? Are they off limits?

- Are there specific areas I should stay clear of? Which areas are not strategically relevant to the business? Which areas should I avoid because they can drag the company into legal or ethical grey areas? Are there any potential minefields that I should not stray into?

- Do the ideas have to be close to our current offerings? Or is it OK to play with ideas in an industry or domain that the company is not currently operating in? How about adjacencies? How about ideas that could potentially cannibalize a part of our current business?

- What about fuzzy projects? What if it's just not possible to quantify an idea's potential with any degree of reliability? If all I have is a strong gut feeling that "there's something there," is that enough to explore it further, or should I stick to ideas that can be reliably modeled in a spreadsheet?

- How much risk is acceptable? Should I prioritize safe bets over high-reward, high-risk projects? How do I gauge the relationship between risk and rewards? How much can I decide for myself under the radar, and when does it become necessary to get approvals?

- Who can I collaborate with? Is it OK to talk to external people? What about partners? Can we discuss ideas openly with partners, or is that a strategic no-go? Should I stay within the department, or is it fine to chat with other business units?

What these questions really highlight are the various ways in which a lone, unguided innovator can create a mess. In the absence of guidance, more cautious employees will simply not do anything, whereas more gung-ho people just might charge ahead and start creating trouble.

Of course, if someone comes up with a specific idea, she may come to you and ask these questions directly. The point of providing focus, though, is to *front-load* this guidance or at least the parts of it that can be defined in advance. By sharing the key constraints and pitfalls, you can accomplish the dual aim of avoiding trouble, while also increasing the chance that people come up with good ideas in the first place.

3. Shift the Search Space: Which New Areas Should People Look at?

So far, we have talked about clarifying objectives and setting good boundaries for innovators. The final point is of a more exploratory nature and points out that, beyond focusing the search for ideas, innovation architects must also seek out new and unexplored areas of the business, in what we call *shifting the search space*. To illustrate this idea, consider the following story, experienced by a leader we know.

You may not have heard of Glenn Rogers or his company Go Travel, but you have almost certainly encountered his products. Go Travel—previously called Design Go—is one of the world's leading manufacturers of travel accessories. If you travel a lot, you have probably bought an inflatable headrest or a power adapter from one of its airport stands. Like many other companies, Go Travel's innovation efforts are focused on developing new consumer products. Once new product ideas have been conceptualized, Rogers has a small team of four people who regularly meet to see which ideas have the most merit to move forward—whether a new design for a headrest, a new way of packaging earplug sets, a better way to manufacture them, or perhaps an entirely new kind of gadget to serve the needs of travelers. Following this approach, in a typical year, Go Travel puts about thirty-five new products on the market.

At one point, however, Rogers and his team did something interesting: they *shifted the search space*, looking beyond products toward new areas in which to innovate. Go Travel's products are stocked on small stands in airports and department stores, and traditionally the individual store owner or his staff would decide on how the products were placed on each stand. Rogers and his team started to wonder if they could do something in that space. As Rogers told us:

> What happened was, we stepped away from thinking about products for a second, and started asking questions about the placement of our products. We knew that the retailers stocked our stands based on some combination of common sense and convenience—but the practices differed from store to store, and nobody did any kind of systematic analysis of how the placement affected sales. So we started asking ourselves, could we innovate in *that* space? Could we, for instance, create some kind of software that could help us determine the best way to place the products?

At the time, the idea seemed interesting to Rogers, but also a little odd. Investing in computer programs to optimize whether product X should be placed on the left or the right side of product Y is the kind of thing that retailing giants like Walmart does. But then, Walmart also sends up its own satellites. Walmart is so big that even a minor cost savings of a few dollars per store can justify major investments, and it has countless items in its product portfolio. The notion that Rogers's company could get any serious benefit from analyzing product placement, let alone convince the retailers to follow its recommendations, seemed a little far-fetched. And Rogers's direct customers—from department stores to airport retailers—certainly hadn't expressed any interest in a service of this nature.

Nonetheless, Rogers found the idea interesting enough to pursue it and ended up paying a UK software developer to build an application for it. As it turned out, the results were much better than anyone had expected:

> Our first major success came within weeks of going live. We identified that our largest UK client could in fact get one extra product onto the space already allocated to us. With five products to a hook, eight hundred retail stores and a sell-through rate in excess of ten times a year, this one insight paid for the entire cost of developing the software. Today, not one of our customers manages the placement themselves; that's become fully automated across the forty-five countries we sell in, and has helped us increase our business fivefold.

Innovation Is a Searchlight

As Glenn Rogers's story highlights, when leaders direct the search for innovation to new areas, it can create extraordinary results. This is something innovation architects can do deliberately. The choice of focus area for innovation can be thought of as a *searchlight* that the leader decides where to point. The metaphor is a useful thinking tool because it conveys several ideas about guiding the search for innovation:

- Your job, as a leader, is to point the beam in the right direction, so your people can look in the right areas.

- Like attention, a searchlight works best when it is focused. If you widen the beam too much, trying to look everywhere at the same time, you can't really see clearly.

- By default, the searchlight tends to point squarely toward one area, such as new product development. By regularly moving the beam, leaders can ensure that their people explore new areas of the business that might harbor great innovation potential.

As you consider where to point the searchlight, we recommend using some kind of model or framework, so the search becomes systematic. In appendix A, we list a few models that you can use to map your business model and identify new or underexplored areas to target.

Conclusion: Suggested Action Items

This chapter has described the first keystone behavior, helping people *focus*. To increase the likelihood that your people will look for ideas in the right places, and do so with the focus necessary to make progress, you can:

- Clarify the strategic purpose of innovating. What specific outcome or goal would most benefit your business? What would make a significant difference? What would not?

- Consider again the list of questions that employees face when they try to innovate, listed in the section on defining the sandbox. What are the key constraints for *your* business? Is there a clearly defined sandbox that people can innovate within?

- Is there a very specific, important problem that you can define for your people, directing them to solve it? As Previdoli did at Lonza, try to experiment with being very directive in the search and see how it works.

- Think through the various aspects of your business model, your value chain, and your company's interactions with various stakeholders. Are there any areas where people have *not* been looking for innovation that might prove fruitful?

- Finally, are the objectives, the constraints, and the search spaces communicated or shared with people in a way they can understand and use in daily life?

CHAPTER 3

CONNECT

HOW TO HELP PEOPLE GET
HIGH-IMPACT IDEAS

INSIGHT COMES FROM THE OUTSIDE

Leaders must help people connect to customers,
colleagues, and beyond

As Bernard D. Sadow, a forty-four-year-old luggage company executive, came back from vacation in Aruba, he had an insight that would eventually make him president of his business, create a profitable two-year monopoly space for his company, and secure a handsome royalty payment for him for decades to come. The insight occurred to Sadow as he was standing in the flight transfer customs area in Puerto Rico's airport, along with his wife, his two kids, and two heavy, twenty-seven-inch suitcases. Then, the magical moment happened: an airport employee walked past him, effortlessly rolling a large piece of machinery on a wheeled trolley.

Sadow looked at the trolley. Then he looked at his two suitcases. Finally, he looked his wife and said the immortal words: "Now that's what we need: wheels on luggage."

Sadow's story contains several lessons about innovation, but the single most remarkable fact is this: it happened in 1970. Now, in 1970, you might recall, mankind had managed to put wheels on a lot of different things: on toys, bikes, cars, airplanes, and, for that matter, on the lunar rover that NASA's upcoming Apollo 15 mission would launch some 250,000 miles through empty space to cruise around the surface of the moon. But try to find a *suitcase* with wheels and you'd be fresh out of luck until 1972, when department store Macy's first started selling Sadow's invention. Considering that the wheel was invented in approximately 3,500 BC, an alien observer would have no option but to conclude that for about 5,472 years, mankind apparently *liked* carrying heavy things around.*

The story gets stranger still. The wheeled suitcase that Sadow came up with wasn't like the smoothly gliding boxes we use today. Rather, it was a regular, old-fashioned suitcase with four small wheels and a little strap to drag it, like a stubborn dog on a leash. The suitcase was so wobbly and cumbersome that Sadow eventually came up with a separate invention to stabilize it, namely, training wheels for suitcases. It wasn't until 1987—fifteen years later—that a pilot, Robert Plath, deigned to come up with an improvement, the Rollaboard. He did this by (1) turning the suitcase on its side, and (2) adding a telescope

---

*Sadow was not the first person to come up with the *idea* of rolling suitcases; for one, in 1958, D. Dudley Bloom, an inventor, attempted to get his boss at the Atlantic Luggage Company to approve a similar product. However, Sadow is considered the father of the rolling suitcase because he was the first to *implement* the idea. As you will recall from our definition, it ain't innovation unless you create results.

pole to make it easier to drag. Plath went on to found a luggage company and got rich off his invention as well.*

Finding the Quick, Big Wins

When looking for good ideas, people tend to look toward two things: *future trends* and *new technology*. What are the trends in the marketplace? What will our customers demand in three years' time? What can we do with the new social media platforms? What will happen when RFID tags become popular, when our customers go mobile, when biotech goes mainstream, or when the coming "Internet of things" becomes a reality?

Certainly, those are important questions. But Sadow's story is a potent reminder that not all ideas are about the future; in fact, some of the most useful ideas can come from the *past*. New technology, while exciting, is inherently risky and ill understood, and the future is an erratically moving target. In comparison, consider the rolling suitcase. It solved a consumer pain point that had been poorly served for years, if not decades; it did so by using the world's oldest technology, the wheel, and it helped its creator make a killing in the market.** Which brings us to the core question of this chapter: how can you help your people get more of *those* ideas?

---

*If you want to share this story, we have made a slide set available on our web site, www.IAsUsual.com.

**Prior to the invention of the wheeled suitcase, the problem of transporting luggage was not so much unsolved as it was *poorly* solved. Luggage had typically been handled by porters, but the space constraints of airport terminals made this solution impractical. Wheeled carts were also available, but as a stand-alone product that consumers had to strap their suitcases onto. It was those inferior solutions that the wheeled suitcase replaced.

Recombinant Innovation

The answer relates to the second keystone behavior: helping people *connect*. Due to a large body of research, we now have a pretty clear answer to the question of where new ideas come from: they come when people are systematically exposed to *new, external input*. No matter how bright people are, if they sit and move in the same worlds every day, getting the same kind of input as everybody else, chances are they won't get original ideas. On the other hand, when people regularly expose themselves to new ideas and places—when they meet new people, spend time with their customers, stay in other countries, are exposed to new industries, experience different cultures, read new books, study new fields, or even just leave the office—they dramatically increase their chances of getting better ideas.

The reason has to do with the nature of a new idea. As Andrew Hargadon, author of *How Breakthroughs Happen*, points out, most ideas are created through what he calls *recombinant innovation*: that is, they are the result of combining two or more old, existing ideas. As an example, consider this classic story, told by the creativity guru Edward de Bono, about how a team of medical researchers came to understand a specific feature of the human kidney:

> For many years physiologists could not understand the purpose of the long loops in the kidney tubules: it was assumed that the loops had no special function and were a relic of the way the kidney had evolved. Then one day an engineer looked at the loops and at once recognized that they could be part of a counter-current multiplier, a well-known engineering device for increasing the concentration of solutions. In this instance a fresh look from outside provided an answer to something that had been a puzzle for a long time.

The story presents a textbook example of how the involvement of someone with different knowledge can help solve difficult problems. The engineer didn't have any understanding of physiology, nor did he have any kind of training in the medical field. Compared to the level of knowledge of the physiologists, he was, for all intents and purposes, an idiot. But that is entirely irrelevant, because the engineer had something far more important: *he had a piece of the physiologists' puzzle in his head*. As a result, their meeting resulted in what we tend to call a breakthrough.

Innovation Is a Puzzle

There is more to the story than this, however. We tend to think that creative breakthroughs come from creative thinkers. But as the creativity researcher Robert Weisberg pointed out, responding to de Bono's story, there is something funny about this particular breakthrough, because when you think about it, *who was being creative?* The physiologists, for one, weren't doing any creative thinking; they were just handed the solution. The engineer who saw the tubules, on the other hand, did not have a brilliant flash of insight either; he just saw something he recognized. The breakthrough, in other words, didn't occur inside anyone's head. It occurred *in the space between them*, in the bringing together of a problem with a solution. The real creative force, if there was one, was the person who made it possible for the engineer and the physiologists to interact, that is, the architect behind the meeting.

This kind of creative space is what the innovation expert Frans Johansson calls *intersections*. In his books *The Medici Effect* and *The Click Moment*, Johansson describes how radical ideas spring from the meeting of different people, disciplines, and viewpoints. Creative spaces or intersections are important because they work as marketplaces for problems and solutions, allowing them to find each other. Sometimes, the creative space is inside our heads, as one individual travels to different places and gathers new input, storing and mixing them within the confines of his or her mind. Other times, the creative spaces are physical, as in de Bono's story. At still other times, the creative spaces are virtual, residing on web sites, intranets, and various other types of idea markets. The essence is that, for companies seeking to innovate, their creation and continued usage are far too important to be left to coincidence. They must be deliberately engineered into the workplace, as part of the architecture of insight.

Three Ways to Connect People to the Outside

The secret to getting original ideas, then, turns out to be relatively simple. You essentially need to think of an idea as a *puzzle*, one whose pieces are distributed across different parts of the world. Some pieces are in books, reports, and other artifacts; others are lying dormant in data, waiting to be discovered; still others are stored in the minds of other people, waiting to be brought together in the mind of an innovator. The role of the innovation architect is not to find these pieces, but to create an architecture of insight—that is, an infrastructure of spaces, places, and connections—that enables people to encounter them. You need, in brief, to build creative spaces into the weave of the workplace. In this chapter, we explain how you can do that, focusing on three particular types of connections:

1. Connecting people to the world of the customer

2. Connecting people to their colleagues

3. Connecting people to new, unrelated worlds

1. Connect People to the Customer's World

If you are looking for valuable, quick-win ideas, your current customers are never a bad place to start. But connecting your employees to the customer is not enough. *How* people engage with the customer matters a lot, because not all approaches are equally likely to yield good ideas.

To test your own intuition on this issue, rate the six idea-generation methods in figure 3-1, taken from a recent study

FIGURE 3-1

Six select methods for generating ideas

☐	External idea contest	☐	Ethnographic research (direct observation of consumers in their natural setting)
☐	Invite external finished product designs	☐	Customer focus groups for problem detection
☐	External submission of ideas	☐	Customer visit teams

Source: adapted from Robert Cooper and Scott Edgett, "Ideation for Product Innovation: What Are the Best Methods?" *PDMA Visions Magazine*, March 2008.

of new product development. For each method, put either a plus or a minus in the box, depending on whether you think the method is generally a good or a bad way to generate valuable new ideas. Write down your answers before you read on.

The methods are from a study of product innovation in which researchers Robert G. Cooper and Scott Edgett asked a hundred sixty companies to evaluate eighteen different idea-generation methods, indicating how fruitful they had found them to be. The list you just evaluated comprised the three best-rated and the three worst-rated methods of all eighteen methods. The three rated most fruitful are:

1. Ethnographic research

2. Customer-visit teams

3. Customer focus groups for problem detection

At the other end of the scale are the three *lowest*-ranked methods of the eighteen methods the study reviewed:

16. Invite external finished product designs

17. External submission of ideas

18. External idea contest

A single study should not, of course, be considered a truth carved in stone; the results might have been different had the study looked beyond product innovation. But taken as a broad indication, there is an interesting pattern hidden in the top-versus-bottom comparison.

Immersion and Problem Finding

In brief, the methods rated least fruitful are all based on the assumption that *customers can get the idea for you*. In this view, there is no particular need for your people to be innovative; they just need to act as idea receivers. As the survey indicated, this is not a viable philosophy. By and large, customers will not provide you with original ideas. As the example of the wheeled suitcase indicated, people can be surprisingly blind to even major pain points related to your product or service.* (See also the box "MyStarbucksIdea: Do Customers Get Original Ideas?")

In comparison, the three top-rated methods represent a different and more potent philosophy of hunting for insights. In particular, ethnography, customer visits, and problem-oriented focus groups share two things. First of all, people are not looking for ideas; they are looking for *problems*. By listening to the frustrations of clients and, more importantly, examining the way they do things, the shortcuts they take and the pain points they encounter, your people will start to notice new opportunities. To produce an idea with immediate appeal in the marketplace, the single best thing you can do is to identify a significant *unmet need or problem* that customers share, like when Sadow spotted the need for making luggage easier to move.

---

*There is an important exception to this, namely, lead user research, a method developed by MIT's Eric von Hippel, in which companies seek out special, advanced users of their products and look at how they modify the company's products to suit their needs. While the method is generally considered to be fruitful, it does hinge on the ability to identify the right set of lead users to study, and it still requires your people to get immersed.

MyStarbucksIdea: Do Customers Get Original Ideas?

Early in 2008, Starbucks launched MyStarbucksIdea.com, a crowdsourcing web site where its customers could submit ideas and vote on the ones they liked. The site received lots of media attention, and people certainly picked up the gauntlet; one year after the platform launched, they had submitted more than 70,000 ideas; that number is now more than 100,000. To date, from that vast roaring sea of suggestions, Starbucks has implemented slightly over 200 ideas in total. Of every 500 ideas, 499 were discarded or put on hold.

Setting aside the question of what expectations their users may have had, the low implementation ratio is not problematic. It is simply a reflection of the fact that *most ideas are bad ideas*. But looking at the select few ideas that *were* implemented, the question beckons: were they any good? From this massive river of customer ideas, did Starbucks produce any high-impact innovations? Here is a choice selection of the ideas that were implemented; judge their impact potential for yourself.

- "BRING BACK CHOCOLATE CINNAMON BREAD!!!"

- "Taste Testing Events."

- "Mocha Coconut Frappucino!!!! Please bring it back!!!"

- "Open a Starbucks in Norway."

- "Please feature Zee Avi's Album—The Asian Ella!"

If you look at the more than two hundred ideas Starbucks decided to implement, it becomes clear that a lot of them are requests to bring back products Starbucks had already invented internally, but then discontinued. The list also includes some more novel-sounding ideas, such as the idea for a mobile payment app. But overall, the list is arguably characterized by a striking absence of ideas that Starbucks could not have gotten itself with a lot less effort.

In our view, MyStarbucksIdea illustrates the fact that a well-executed campaign to crowdsource ideas from customers can be an excellent *marketing* tool. It certainly was for Starbucks, as it garnered lots of positive media acclaim and managed to engage many of its customers.* As the many "bring back product X!" ideas attest to, it can also be a way to listen to the market, in addition to what Starbucks would already have known from its sales data. But in terms of getting original, high-impact ideas, in line with what Cooper and Edgett's survey indicated, idea crowdsourcing efforts like MyStarbucksIdea are probably of little value relative to the investment they require. (Of course, Starbucks might disagree with this opinion, as will surely the world's lovers of chocolate cinnamon bread.)

---

*Social media campaigns can backfire, though. In January 2012, McDonald's launched a social media campaign on Twitter, encouraging people to tweet their favorite stories about McDonald's using the hashtag, #McDStories. The campaign was shut down hours later, as the customers mainly opted to share tweets like this one, by @SkipSullivan: "One time I walked into McDonalds and I could smell Type 2 diabetes floating in the air and I threw up."

Second, when looking for insights, your people need to be *immersed:* they must be in direct, personal, and prolonged contact with the customer. Unmet needs will rarely reveal themselves through e-mails or similar "thin" channels. Sadow didn't get the idea for the rolling suitcase by sitting in his office, occasionally reading letters from customers; instead, he was out in the world, *acting* like his customers. By immersing yourself in somebody else's world, walking in their shoes, and feeling their pain, you start seeing the important nuances of their lives. As Erich Joachimsthaler, author of *Hidden in Plain Sight* and founder of the consumer insights company Vivaldi Partners puts it:

> The typical problem with corporate innovation is that it tends to take an *inside-out* perspective: it's driven internally, by either the R&D department or the marketing people. If it's the techies that drive ideas, you end up with lots of new gadgets that nobody, least of all consumers, knows what to do with. The marketing department, on the other hand, is theoretically speaking closer to the consumers—but the key problem with marketing people is that they spend too much time trying to *be understood*, and too little time trying to *understand*. To succeed with innovation, you need to adopt a true *outside-in* perspective, and that starts with getting a detailed, in-depth understanding of what consumers actually do with the 1,440 minutes that their days are comprised of. Without that, you are innovating with a barn-sized blind spot.

How to Increase People's Exposure to Customers

Cooper and Edgett's study, which is available online, provides a number of suggestions on how to search for new ideas.

(See also "Focus Groups: Good or Bad?") However, instigating larger-scale efforts, such as ethnographic studies or customer-visit teams, might be beyond your means. Fortunately, less can also do it. Here are some simple, structural ways of increasing your people's exposure to customers:

- Some employees will already be regularly in touch with customers. Can you find a way of leveraging that existing connection?

- Can you give your salespeople some basic training in observation, along with a simple reward system for sharing interesting insights?

- Can you reward your call-center people for submitting observations about a frequent or interesting customer frustration, for instance, by promising them a small share of the cost savings if any of their ideas are acted upon?

- Can you have people take cellphone pictures if they witness a surprising use of your products, for example when customers make modifications to the design or use the product in a way it wasn't intended for? (See, for instance, www.ThereIFixedIt.com, where people upload improvised fixes to various products.) Can they film a quick video of a customer facing an overlooked problem, such as "wrap rage," the term for the frustration people feel when factory packaging is hard to open? (For a great example of this, see Rebecca Greenfield's article on The Atlantic's web site, "Google Doesn't Get the Importance of Gadget Packaging.")

- Can you find ways of helping your *other* employees connect with customers, not just once but regularly? Could you, for instance, invite one or two customers to be part of some internal meetings?

- Can you find other ways of regularly bringing customers inside the company? One company we worked with hosted various customer events at their office. Can you do something similar?

Your end customers are clearly an important group, but this approach works on other stakeholders as well. If you head up an internal service function like Jordan Cohen's pfizerWorks, your "customers" can be your own company's employees, for example, the people in the field or even the people in the next office. If you deal with business-to-business relationships, maybe you need to spend more time with your suppliers or other partners. As we cover later in this chapter, you can sometimes find new revenue sources by looking outside the existing market and connecting your people to new, unrelated worlds.

2. Connect People to Their Colleagues

A few years ago, the Neoresins unit of the global science company DSM had a problem with one of its experimental products, a new and ecologically friendly type of adhesive known as E-850. The new adhesive was used to glue thin layers of wood together, creating laminated boards for table surfaces and similar items. The problem was that when a lacquer was subsequently applied, the laminate would start fraying at the edges.

After two years of trying and failing to solve the problem internally, three of DSM's people, Steven Zwerink, Erik Pras,

Focus Groups: Good or Bad?

Some innovation experts don't advocate focus groups; Innosight's Scott Anthony, for instance, simply advises people to "avoid focus groups like the plague." Others find them to be useful tools, as indicated by Cooper and Edgett's study.

We tend to side with the focus group detractors. Focus groups, especially if conducted by trained interviewers, can be useful in identifying some of the more obvious problems that customers face, as well as giving you some insight into the rhetoric people use about your products. However, they will also give you a lot of *bad* information, and this is not just a question of whether people are lying. What's more fascinating is that studies of human behavior have shown that people often are simply *fundamentally unaware* of the real reasons for their actions, yet if asked, they will still fabricate a reason (and believe in it). A relevant example is the power of architecture that we advocate in this book. Countless studies have shown that people are heavily influenced by context, but when asked, they almost always deny that the context they were in influenced their actions. Observational methods, although slightly more cumbersome to organize, will tell you how people *actually* behave, which can be mind-bogglingly different from how they say they behave.

and Theo Verweerden, decided to run an experiment: they created a PowerPoint presentation describing the problem, promised a cash prize of €10,000 to the person who could solve it, and then went public with the slide set, sharing it via various social media. Within a few weeks, five different people provided input that, when combined, solved the problem for DSM, allowing it to put E-850 on the market. (The five contributors shared the prize money equally.)

The overall arc of the E-850 story is similar to many other success stories that have come from the move toward open innovation: if you broadcast your problem to the world, you may find that someone out there has already solved it or can at least provide a critical piece of the puzzle. However, in the context of finding insights, what makes the DSM story particularly interesting is the additional twist it offered to the narrative. As the team discovered, of the five people who helped solve the problem, *three already worked for DSM*. For two years, the people in the Neoresins unit had been struggling with a problem that some of their own colleagues could have helped them solve, had they only known about it earlier.

Building Internal Creative Spaces

As the DSM story shows, the keystone behavior of connecting is not just about reaching outside the organization. To find useful insights, sometimes all you have to do is connect people to their own colleagues.

The power of internal connections can be a great starting point for leaders to build an architecture of insight. After all, it can be a lot less complicated to connect your employees to their colleagues than to the outside world, and there are also fewer thorny questions about intellectual property. Next, we share some examples of how you can work to connect people internally.

Using Physical Spaces

If you seek to foster more connections among your people, an obvious starting point is the *actual* architecture of the workplace: the bricks-and-mortar, office-divider kind. Steve Jobs's restroom relocation, described in chapter 1, is a memorable example, but similar cross-fertilizing effects can be achieved more modestly. Sometimes, simple acts like moving the coffee machine, creating a breakout space with a soft sofa in a broad hallway, or pooling the office printers in a single location can make people interact across departments. Or think about how you can make existing rendezvous points, such as smoking areas, more likely to foster interaction. As the members of your local tobacco tribe take to the streets for a fresh breath of tar, can you find ways to cater to their interaction?

If you decide to experiment by moving things around in the office, we have two notes of caution. First, be careful making universal or hard-to-reverse changes to the workplace. After the initial and enthusiastic embrace of the open-office movement that scourged the corporate landscape in the 1990s, it became clear that the concept didn't always deliver on its promises and occasionally created whole new types of problems. Before making significant changes to the office layout, read Anne-Laure Fayard and John Weeks's article, "Who Moved My Cube?" in which they detail how open workplaces must provide "permission triggers" for interaction as well as hit a balance between proximity and privacy.

Second, even with minor tweaks to the workplace, make sure to explain to people why you're doing it, or better yet, ask *them* to find ways to do it. Randomly removing a well-frequented watercooler without a word of explanation is a great way to make people feel like totalitarian-state lab animals. As with many (if not all) initiatives of this nature, employee involvement is preferable to autocratic decision making. (For a discussion of creative spaces that are virtual instead of physical, see the sidebar "Online Suggestion Boxes: Do They Work?")

Online Suggestion Boxes: Do They Work?

A currently popular innovation tool is the introduction of web-based idea management platforms. At their most basic, idea management platforms are online versions of the classic suggestion box, giving employees everywhere an easy way to submit their ideas to the company. Most offer additional features such as peer voting, discussion forums and similar.

We recommend being cautious before you buy into such solutions. We have seen several examples of companies that have benefited strongly from them, but equally often we have seen managers severely disappointed by the lack of results. To date, the currently available data on these kinds of solutions also suggests that a significant proportion of users are not satisfied with their performance.

In our view, there are two particular pitfalls. The first one is pointed out by London Business School professor Julian Birkinshaw in his book *Reinventing Management*: software tools can be great for *collecting* ideas, but by and large, they tend to be poor platforms for the subsequent *collaboration* on those ideas, which is typically the phase where most of the work needs to happen. The second pitfall is an extension of that insight, shared by Mark Turrell, former CEO of the ideation software company Imaginatik. The problem is that the software platform itself, while looking nice and shiny, is only one part of the solution. For the total system to work, you also need to build new organizational routines, processes, and incentive systems around the software platform. If you don't get all these things right, all you have done is to add another IT project to the company—surely not what the doctor would have ordered for anyone.*

*Having said that, the field is still in its tumultuous early years, and we think it likely that we will see much better versions of these tools in the future, as the current Cambrian explosion of software solutions eventually settles into a more stable landscape of viable, time-tested solutions. In particular, we believe online platforms that are aimed at connecting people and broadcasting problems or questions hold significant promise. Should you be looking for a managerial experiment to run, trying out one of these tools might lead to some interesting learning, if not necessarily guaranteed short-term results.

Bring Outsiders onto the Team

New teams aren't formed every day, but when they are, it's an excellent opportunity to get new insights into the local ecosystem. When Jordan Cohen built pfizerWorks, he knew that he needed help from someone in the field to get the service working as it should. So when he had the chance to bring another person on board, he didn't pick an insider, that is, a local colleague from the New York office. Instead, he went out of his way to hire Tanya Carr-Waldron, a senior field person with twenty years of experience dealing with the frontlines of the company. In addition to the credibility and the network that Carr-Waldron brought to the project, she played a crucial role in getting all the details right in how the service worked, something Cohen would have been incapable of doing on his own.

Marc Granger did something similar on a smaller scale. As he worked with his management team, discussing how to drive innovation at NutroFoods Belgium, he deliberately included his personal assistant in the meetings, who gave the team a firsthand perspective on how employees felt about the company. It would perhaps have been simpler and more convenient to have only the management team at the meetings—some leaders feel uneasy about involving employees in managerial conversations—but it would also have robbed them of some crucial knowledge about the company. As a leader, can you have your people include someone with a different perspective when the next project team is formed?

Make Your Meetings More Cross-Functional

One of the most underrated creativity tools is the simple act of having more cross-functional meetings. When one company we worked in created new campaigns for its products, the marketing department started on its own and invited the other departments later on in the process, once it was time to execute the campaigns. As a result, it ended up sticking to some fairly traditional and not all that effective solutions. But all that changed when the department started involving more people earlier.

With the new approach, it would invite people from the other departments to participate from the beginning of the process, making them part of the problem-finding phase. As a result, the company started inventing and executing some innovative and highly successful new marketing campaigns.

To be sure, these benefits didn't come without some investments in time and effort. Inviting other people into the process early on meant that the meetings got longer, and the marketers had to spend more time explaining things to the outsiders that their same-department colleagues took for granted. The cost of increased involvement is more time spent on coordination and communication; and longer meetings are never popular with anyone. But the results can be worthwhile, making this a good candidate for experimentation (if you are not doing it already).

Keeping It Simple: Lunches with Strangers

If your company is like most other workplaces, the way people behave around lunchtime is extremely predictable. Once people have stocked up on their penne al arrabiata, an incredibly powerful gravitational pull brings them to sit down and chat with the people *they already know*, often at the exact same table where they sat yesterday. There is only one force of nature stronger than this social tractor beam of the cafeteria; that's the one dictating that, on a bus, you never, ever sit next to a stranger if there are two free seats elsewhere.

A French company we worked with decided to change that habit. The company housed several subdivisions in the same office building, and the managers of those divisions only had one monthly meeting to coordinate, with the result that nobody really knew what was going on in the other parts of the business. So in one meeting, the leader came up with a simple idea: one day a week, people on the team would have a private one-on-one lunch with one of the other team members. In order not to invade his team's break time with work, the lunch didn't have to be professional; there was no agenda, so they were free to chat about whatever they liked. The idea worked well, and the practice soon spread, with the department managers setting up a similar system for their employees.

We won't claim that this practice changed the company; as far as we know, people did not come up with an industry-changing idea as they polished off their escargots and baguettes. The real reason we share this story is to point out that *the solution doesn't have to be complex*. Some of the tips in this chapter may at first seem too laborious to undertake, but if so, try to scale down the idea to a level where it seems doable. It is almost always possible to find ways to connect people to their colleagues.

3. Connect People to New, Unrelated Worlds

Colleagues and current customers are important and accessible sources of new insights, but they are not the only ones. Sometimes, to find the most interesting ideas, you must help people look for puzzle pieces in *unrelated* worlds, places that do not have any obvious relevance to your business. By having people connect regularly to new, unrelated worlds, you can help them increase their personal stock of puzzle pieces, making it more likely that someone will have an original, value-creating insight. In some situations, like Sadow's observation of the wheeled airport trolley in Puerto Rico, a random piece of input from the outside will help people think differently about their own products and services. In other situations, they will discover that they hold solutions to *other* people's problems, solutions that might be turned into a new service, converting noncustomers into new customers.

Steffen Kragh, CEO and president of the large Nordic media group, Egmont, shared an example illustrating the second situation. TV 2, a leading Norwegian broadcasting subsidiary of Egmont, had a small unit that forecasted weather; it was run as a cost center that allowed Egmont's television channels to deliver accurate weather reports. However, by scanning the external world and looking for new opportunities, the people working in the unit discovered that there was someone out there who was willing to pay for their services, namely the Nordic hydroelectrical power industry and the oil industry, for which more accurate local weather data had significant value. Based on that discovery, the weather forecasting unit became an independent for-profit company, StormGeo, founded by TV 2 and chief meteorologist and TV presenter Siri Kalvig. Today, the company provides services globally to sectors such as oil and gas, renewable energy, shipping, media, and aviation. Similarly, by connecting your people to the outside, you can enable them to discover new opportunities and turn noncustomers into customers.

Here are some ways to help people connect to the outside:

- Use social media. The Internet offers endless rows of windows into new worlds. Web sites like www.ted.com offer short videos with a host of interesting people and ideas, ideal for viewing while commuting. The MIX community (short for Management Innovation eXchange) started by Gary Hamel and Polly LaBarre, contains hundreds of great stories about corporate innovations. Blogs like www.InnovationExcellence.com, run by Braden Kelly, Rowan Gibson, and Julie Anixter, offer frequent doses of fresh thinking. Twitter and similar services deliver instant inspiration. Can you get some of your people to use these services?

- Create a habit of trend spotting. As part of your weekly meetings, have one person deliver a one-slide, two-minute presentation on an interesting new trend or idea she has encountered. Rotate this assignment to get everybody looking outside for new ideas.

- Use books and articles. In our MBA courses at IESE, we have each student read a (different) book during the course and write a short summary of the key ideas. Consider doing something similar, asking people to select books or articles about industries other than your own.

- Hire interesting interns. When hiring for regular positions, chances are that your hiring criteria emphasize industry knowledge, for good reasons. But hiring interns can allow for more experimentation. In one company we worked with, an intern turned out to be an expert on social media, so the leadership asked the intern to tour the company and give presentations on the topic. Can you hire interns who bring new knowledge into the company?

Conclusion: Suggested Action Items

This chapter highlighted the second keystone behavior, helping people *connect*. To increase the likelihood that your people will find high-impact ideas, you can:

- Share the story of the rolling suitcase (the slides are available on our web site: www.IAsUsual.com). Remind people to look for ideas that use old technology and solve existing pain points. Ask what product or service we should have invented *three years ago*, but which nobody in our industry has yet come up with?

- Find systematic ways of getting people close to the customer. Can you tweak existing patterns of interaction, such as sales visits, to make them more fruitful? Can you bring customers inside the company?

- Get people to connect *internally*, interacting regularly with colleagues from other departments. Can you create simple routines that foster formal and informal communication? Can you involve people in creating these habits, sharing the dual purpose of innovating and getting to know their colleagues better?

- Help people connect to the outside as part of their regular work. Look for the opportunity to expose people to new ideas and help them form new personal habits that deliver fresh thinking and inspiration every day.

CHAPTER 4

TWEAK

HOW TO HELP PEOPLE IMPROVE THEIR IDEAS

FIRST IDEAS ARE FLAWED

Leaders must make people test, challenge, and
reframe their ideas repeatedly

At the moment of conception, all ideas seem perfect. If you've ever had an "aha" moment, you know that feeling of pure, majestic *rightness* when new ideas present themselves.

Sadly, that feeling is an illusion. Most ideas ultimately turn out to be bad ideas, and to make it worse, even *good* ideas are almost never perfect to begin with. Quite the contrary: as demonstrated by the work of Rita McGrath, Steve Blank, and others, chances are that *the first version of any given idea will be flawed*. Or as Scott Anthony puts it, innovators must assume that their plans are partly right *and* partly wrong and then work hard at figuring out which part of the plan is wrong.

The problem is, unless people have prior experience with innovation, they are likely to trust too much in the perfection of their initial ideas. At the risk of oversimplification, many people assume that innovation works more or less like the model shown in figure 4-1.

FIGURE 4-1

Innovation model (oversimplified)

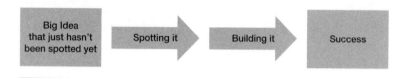

In this model, the role division is conceptually simple. First and foremost, you need a genius: somebody who comes up with a brilliant idea. Then you need some hands-on "doers," people who are strong in execution and can bring the idea to market without diluting or destroying the brilliance. This model may work for minor improvements, but in the majority of cases, what the picture really looks like is shown in figure 4-2.

FIGURE 4-2

Innovation model (in reality)

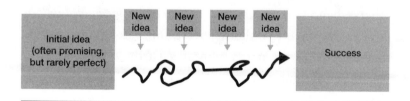

Successful innovations, in other words, are not found; they are *developed*. One part of this development process is the ongoing improvement of the actual product, service, or process that people are creating. But, crucially, it is not just the solution that tends to develop. What will also change is the *understanding of the problem or need* that people aim to address with their innovation. In the most radical cases, both the problem and the solution will mutate so much along the way that the finished innovation will have absolutely nothing to do with the original idea. An oft-cited example is that of PayPal. In 1998, when Max Levchin and Peter Thiel started working together, they were trying to invent an encryption system for Palm Pilots and similar devices, helping big companies keep their internal communications secure. Only through a gradual process of experimentation and learning, stretching over many months and several iterations, did they finally identify the real, lucrative problem they could solve: that of making online payments safe and easy.

Two Ways to Help People Make Their Ideas Better

While PayPal is an extreme example of how an idea can change direction, the point applies to more modest innovations as well: to succeed, leaders must help their people engage in the third keystone behavior, constantly *tweaking* their ideas. As people come up with ideas, you have to create routines and processes that help them test and challenge those ideas, quickly and repeatedly.

Effectively, this means that you must have your people do two things:

1. Reframe the problem. Have your people define, analyze, and challenge their understanding of the *problem* or *need* they are addressing.

2. Test the solution. Have people test and prototype their ideas quickly and repeatedly, doing real-world experiments whenever possible.

The two behaviors are not sequential, but should happen side by side, in a highly iterative process. In this chapter, we explain how you can achieve this, starting with the process of reframing the problem.

1. Have People Reframe the Problem

The work of a Hungarian psychologist with the delightful name of Mihaly Csikszentmihalyi led to an understanding of the importance of reframing, also called problem finding or problem diagnosis, in the science of creativity. Csikszentmihalyi and his colleague Jacob Getzels became curious about the nature of creative people: What set effective innovators apart from their less successful peers? Why were they so good at getting clever ideas? What was it about these people and their approach that allowed them to succeed where others had failed? To find out, Csikszentmihalyi and Getzels set out to interview hundreds of successful innovators, picking them from all areas of human endeavor.

As they reviewed their findings, they came to a rather surprising conclusion: none of their subjects were particularly skilled at finding solutions to a given problem. What set them apart was something different: they had the ability to see *the problem itself* in a different way from everybody else. Most people, when faced with a problem, immediately start looking for a solution, just as we do in brainstorm sessions. Csikszentmihalyi and Getzel's subjects were different. They would instead stop and ask themselves: Why is this a problem? Do we understand this issue correctly? Are there other ways of looking at it? Successful innovators are not solution finders; they are expert *problem finders*. They understand that solutions are secondary; the answer they seek rests in the problem itself, and once they fully understand it, the solution will often become evident.*

Two Examples: Flip and Dropbox

To see how people's understanding of the problem they solve is crucial to innovation, consider the following two examples, one a physical product and the other a service.

The first example is of two different video recorders aimed at consumers. One is a classic video recorder, in this case, a Canon. The other is the Flip, an innovation that was launched in 2006

---

*Csikszentmihalyi and Getzels were not the first to recognize that problem finding was important to creativity, but they were the first to show that it also applied to the world of business. Getzels is often credited with the first empirical evidence hailing from the art world; see Mihaly Csikszentmihalyi and Jacob W. Getzels, "The Personality of Young Artists: An Empirical and Theoretical Exploration," *British Journal of Psychology* 64, no. 1 (February 1973). Prior to that, several others had written about the phenomenon, stretching back to the early 20th century with John Dewey's *How We Think* (Lexington, MA: D. C. Heath and Company, 1910). For an academic overview of the research into problem finding, we recommend Mark A. Runco, *Problem Finding, Problem Solving, and Creativity* (New York: Ablex Publishing Corporation, 1994).

by a small start-up. As you look at the two products in the photos in figures 4-3 and 4-4, ask yourself: *What did each company assume about its customers' core problem or need?*

FIGURE 4-3

Classic video recorder—Canon

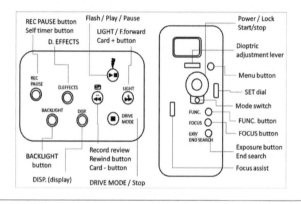

FIGURE 4-4

Innovative video recorder—the Flip

In the first case, Canon seems to have believed that the consumer's biggest problem was to create professional-looking video with just the right image quality; hence, the inclusion of lots of functions and buttons, presumably with a twelve-inch thick instruction manual. In this, Canon took the same approach as most of its competitors at the time.

The creators of the Flip, on the other hand, clearly took aim at a very different problem, namely the *lack of simplicity* that clearly characterized the existing solutions on the market. This alternative understanding of the consumer's problem was quickly proven correct. When the Flip came out, it rapidly started eating into the market for consumer video cameras, and three years later, it was sold to Cisco for $590 million.*

The second example, Dropbox, is an online cloud storage service that lets you sync files across different devices and share them with other people. It was launched in 2007 and quickly became a success story. By 2011, Dropbox had reached annual revenues in the range of $240 million and had been named among the top-five most valuable start-ups, along with Facebook and Twitter. However, Dropbox was far from the first service that allowed people to sync and share files; when it was launched, there were many similar offerings on the market. So the question is, why did a latecomer like Dropbox become so popular? When an anonymous user posted that question on the Q&A web site Quora, one of Quora's users, Michael Wolfe,

---

*Cisco killed the Flip in 2011. Explanations vary, but presumably the two main culprits were (1) a bad fit with Cisco's core competencies; it is not really a consumer products company; and (2) the realization that the Flip itself would soon be outdone, as smartphones became capable of filming decent-quality video. Nonetheless, for the makers of Flip, it proved a pretty good idea.

CEO of Pipewise, gave a perfect answer (see the box, "Why Is Dropbox More Popular Than Other Programs with Similar Functionality?").

Why Is Dropbox More Popular Than Other Programs with Similar Functionality?

Answer by Michael Wolfe, on www.quora.com:

"Well, let's take a step back and think about the sync problem and what the ideal solution for it would do:

- There would be a folder.

- You'd put your stuff in it.

- It would sync.

They built that.

Why didn't anyone else build that? I have no idea.

'But,' you may ask, 'so much more you could do! What about task management, calendaring, customized dashboards, virtual white boarding. More than just folders and files!'

No, shut up. People don't use that crap. They just want a folder. A folder that syncs.

'But,' you may say, 'this is valuable data. Certainly users will feel more comfortable tying their data to Windows Live, Apple's MobileMe, or a name they already know.'

No, shut up. Not a single person on Earth wakes up in the morning worried about deriving more value from their

---

Windows Live login. People already trust folders. And Dropbox looks just like a folder. One that syncs.

'But,' you may say, 'folders are so 1995. Why not leverage the full power of the web? With HTML5 you can drag and drop files, you can build intergalactic dashboards of statistics showing how much storage you are using, you can publish your files as RSS feeds and tweets, and you can add your company logo!'

No, shut up. Most of the world doesn't sit in front of their browser all day. If they do, it is Internet Explorer 6 at work that they are not allowed to upgrade. Browsers suck for these kinds of things. Their stuff is already in folders. They just want a folder. That syncs.

That is what it does."

Wolfe's answer highlights the same point that the Flip did: tweaking an idea isn't just about perfecting the quality of a product or service. Equally important, innovators must *challenge their assumptions about the core problem that their customers are facing*. If they fail to do so and focus exclusively on implementing the first version of their ideas, they can quickly end up running down the wrong path, investing ever more effort in perfecting a solution that targets a wrong or nonexistent problem.

In order to make sure that people don't commit this mistake, you must create simple habits and structures that force them to focus explicitly on the problem, instead of concentrating only on the solution.* Effectively, you must stop them from jumping into action indiscriminately, ensuring that they combine trial-and-error methods with the more analytical work of diagnosing the core problem.

Structured Reframing: Learning from Consultants

To understand how to enable reframing, look at a specific group of companies that have a deep expertise in problem solving: the big consulting firms. Firms like McKinsey & Company, Bain, Booz Allen Hamilton, and the Boston Consulting Group have built vast and thriving business empires on their ability to solve other people's problems. And despite the less than loving feelings that some people have for management consultants in general, the fact is that these firms, when employed correctly, can create lots of value. Which is remarkable considering that consultants know your business less well than you do and that many of the people doing the actual work are fresh out of business school. Put another way, if you ever wondered how on earth a neophyte thirty-something consultant can possibly be worth the kind of money these outfits charge per hour, part of the answer has to do with reframing.

First, McKinsey and its equivalents acutely understand how critical it is to get the problem diagnosis right. As the former

---

*Notably, understanding the real needs or problems is a competitive advantage, but it is not necessarily a source of *sustainable* competitive advantage; for that, further innovations may be needed, along with good old-fashioned efficiency. The Flip, as mentioned earlier, was eventually killed by Cisco, and Dropbox's future prospects may also change as Microsoft, Google, Apple, and others develop their cloud solutions.

McKinsey consultants Ethan M. Rasiel and Paul N. Friga describe in their book *The McKinsey Mind*:

> Every consultant faces the temptation of taking the client's diagnosis of his problem at face value. Resist this temptation. Just as a patient is not always aware of the meaning of his symptoms, so are managers sometimes incorrect in their diagnoses of what ails their organizations. The only way to determine whether the problem you have been given is the real problem is to dig deeper, ask questions, and get the facts. A little skepticism early on in the problem-solving process could save you a lot of frustration further down the road.

Second, McKinsey has made reframing a core part of its organizational architecture, in this case, in the shape of a standardized, rigorous process that all incoming solutions are subjected to, no matter how well defined the problem seems at first. More-senior colleagues carefully train new consultants in this process of mapping a problem and identifying its core drivers. This highly disciplined approach to problem solving (along with the proven capacity to ignore their private lives) make McKinsey-trained graduates sought after by other companies.

Some Simple Methods for Reframing

The problem-solving models that McKinsey and similar firms use are, as a whole, rather elaborate, and in our experience, it can be unrealistic to implement them "as is" in regular workplaces. The good news is that, with the use of a few basic rules, even the most informally run garage start-up can become more systematic about reframing.

- First, explain what reframing is. Most people are not familiar with the concept of problem finding. To start, explain the importance of the method, so they understand why you use this approach. On our website www.IAsUsual.com, we have made some slides available that you can use to convey the basic idea to your people.

- Make people write down the problem. One of the simplest and most efficient reframing tools is to have people write down the problem separately from the solution. If people on a team have different understandings of the problem, which is often the case, this will make it obvious. Once they write down a problem, they will find it far easier to question its current framing, allowing them to probe deeper. (See the box, "Reframing the Problem: Sample Questions.")

- Five Whys. Processes like the Five Whys and root cause analysis can be useful tools for exploring and reframing a problem. Remember though that the point is not necessarily to find one true root cause; rather, make people use the tools to develop alternative perspectives. Another tool, "questorming," developed by Jon Roland makes people brainstorm to find new questions about the problem. The method (which is sometimes called questionstorming) is described online.*

---

*See http://pynthan.com/vri/questorm.htm for a description of Jon Roland's questorming technique. Among other places, QuestionStorming is mentioned in Jeff Dyer, Hal Gregersen, and Clayton Christensen's *The Innovator's DNA: Mastering the Five Skills of Disruptive Innovators* (Boston: Harvard Business Review Press, 2011).

- Jobs to be done. Formalized by Clayton Christensen and Michael Raynor, the jobs-to-be-done framework is a useful analytical tool for reframing. In the vein of marketing professor Theodore Levitt's famous adage that people don't want to buy quarter-inch drills, they want quarter-inch holes, this framework emphasizes that people *hire* products and services to get a particular job (or jobs) done and that innovators must identify that job, including its social and emotional aspects.

- Involve other people. People tend to have specific views of problems based on the tools they have experience using. Communications people see communication problems, HR people see HR problems, and so on. To avoid groupthink, have your people bring somebody with a different perspective into the discussion, and ask *that* person to challenge the framing of the problem.

Reframing the Problem: Sample Questions

Here is a short list of questions you can give people to help them reframe the problem. Remember to make them stick with the problem definition; until people get used to working with the method, they will have a strong propensity to jump into solutions. A good tip is to make people use a shared surface to write on, and use that to visually separate the problem description from the proposed solutions (see also figure 4-5 that follows later).

- What is the exact problem? Write it down, word for word, on a shared surface.

- *Why* is this a problem?

- Is the problem really worth solving?

- Can the problem be described in a completely different way? Try to come up with *at least* 3–4 different ways of describing or interpreting the problem.

- *Who* is it a problem for? Who is it *not* a problem for?

- Who are the other stakeholders?

- How does each stakeholder view the problem? (Go and ask them if possible)

- How do the stakeholders currently solve (or deal with) the problem?

- Could we be wrong about the problem? Could we be looking at a symptom of a deeper problem?

- How exactly does the problem occur, step by step? What actually happens? What does it look like if we film it with a video camera?

- Which observations is our current diagnosis of the problem based on? Are the observations correct? Can they be interpreted in a different way?

- Are there cases where the problem does not occur? What is special about these cases?

- If any solutions have been attempted in the past, why did these fail? Was it only a matter of poor execution, or did the attempted solution address the wrong problem?

- If any new solutions have been proposed, what do these solutions assume about the problem? Is there any evidence that those assumptions are true?

Reframing in Action

If your people are unfamiliar with problem-oriented methods, reframing may seem like just an academic exercise: nice in hindsight but of little use when they are in the middle of a mud-streaked wrestling match with a new idea. This perception is wrong. In our experience, reframing *is* less intuitive than testing, and it takes some effort for people to really grasp the method. But once they do, it can become a useful and time-saving innovation tool.

For a basic example of how to use reframing in practice, consider the following story. Each year, as we teach our MBA course at IESE Business School, we ask our students to implement a real-life innovation project, aimed at improving something about the school itself. A few years ago, one of the teams came up with a simple idea: an awareness campaign that would make people use less paper, specifically by having them print on both sides of the paper instead of on one side. However, before they started planning their campaign, we gave them a simple briefing: first, write down what the problem is.

Why aren't people printing on both sides? Then spend twenty minutes trying to reframe and challenge that problem, coming up with alternative ways of looking at it.

As the team members followed our instructions, they quickly saw that their first take on the problem—lack of awareness—was not a good framing. They came to this realization by thinking about their own behavior: while the team members themselves were very passionate about protecting the environment, *all* had been guilty of printing on only one side of the paper. An awareness campaign would not help, because *the real problem wasn't related to awareness.* The problem was that when people printed things at school, they were almost always *busy,* rushing to meet some deadline. Thus, people simply used the default setting on the printer, which was set to print single-sided. Once the true nature of the problem became clear, the solution was evident: the default setting on all printers was changed to double-sided, immediately achieving a dramatic and lasting reduction in paper usage. Figure 4-5 shows some (non-exhaustive) examples of how the printer problem could be framed, along with the types of solutions each problem framing suggests.

By creating simple routines around reframing, akin to the method we used with our MBA students, people will often make significant inroads on their ideas *before* they expend any effort on implementation. That is the true power of the method: it makes people stop and think before they jump into action and prevents them from running down the wrong path, pursuing a dead-end solution.

However, not all problems will yield to analysis as easily as single-sided printing. As we cover in the next section,

FIGURE 4-5

Observation: Most people print on one side of the paper

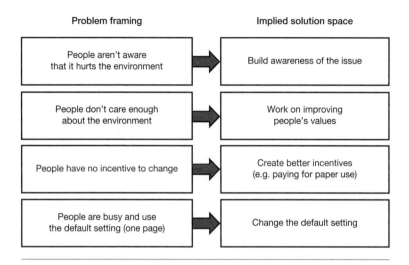

Problem framing	Implied solution space
People aren't aware that it hurts the environment	Build awareness of the issue
People don't care enough about the environment	Work on improving people's values
People have no incentive to change	Create better incentives (e.g. paying for paper use)
People are busy and use the default setting (one page)	Change the default setting

reframing must generally be combined with something else to be effective: rapid real-world testing.

2. Have People Test the Solution: Force Collisions with Reality

Once, on a bright and balmy night in Barcelona, we were chatting with an investor at a professional mixer event for entrepreneurs, when a young MBA student entered the conversation. The student proclaimed that he had spent the last two years writing the *perfect* business plan for a new venture; he asked if the investor would perhaps like to see it. The venture capitalist's first question was, "Have you tested your idea with potential clients?" The MBA student answered that he hadn't found that necessary. After all, he only needed to capture 2 percent of the market in order to break even, and he had been *very* careful about getting his financial projections right. That, predictably, was where the productive part of the conversation ended.

As much as a bit of analysis can prevent people from making ill-considered investments, the fact remains that if you want to learn more about a new idea, nothing beats real-world experiments. As our chance encounter with the MBA student showed, there are certain types of people who love *tinkering*. If given half a chance, they will spend a long time working on their ideas, preferably in complete isolation. They won't test their ideas in the real world because they viscerally *hate* the notion of showing or testing something that's not yet ready.

That, unfortunately, is a surefire way to waste a lot of time and effort. When working on new ideas, innovators should not treat testing as an evaluation tool, applied at the end of the process. Rather, they should use testing and experimenting as *learning* tools, allowing them to tweak their ideas before they have invested too much effort in them. Thus, as a leader, you must force people to test and share their ideas *before* they are ready for prime time. All ideas will have to collide with reality sooner or later. Instead of letting ideas gather momentum for years and *then* meeting an immovable object, ensure that people do quick, miniature collisions with reality, as repeatedly and as early as possible. Two key tweaking habits will help your people do this: rapid prototyping and frequent feedback.

Prehype: Rapid Prototyping in Action

Rapid prototyping is now a standard practice for innovators, particularly among proponents of the so-called *design thinking* approach. Popularized by the influential product design company IDEO, the central idea of prototyping is to build a physical, MacGyver-style mock-up of your product, using adhesive tape and whatever materials you have at hand, and then putting that prototype into the real world to start learning about your idea.

The New York-based innovation firm Prehype, which we have worked with, heavily uses prototyping. A mix between a start-up incubator and a product development coach for big firms, Prehype has worked with companies like Coca-Cola, Intel, Kaplan, and Verizon, assisting them in the pursuit of new ideas. Prehype's most remarkable trait is its core offering: it helps clients create new start-ups in a few months, using the client's own people and ideas. What Prehype adds to that mix are the structures, processes, and support systems necessary to innovate rapidly and successfully, including the strong emphasis on prototyping.* As its founding partner Henrik Werdelin explains:

> Many of our clients aim to develop new online services, and if you let them, they will have endless discussions about value-add, competitive advantage, unique selling points and so on. So to help them get to the core of their ideas, we often make them create a mock website that explains what they do. When you force people to decide what the tagline on their website should say, using seven words

---

*Effectively, Prehype sells innovation architecture as a service. Their business model is described in our case study, "Prehype: Intrapreneurship as a service," available at IESE Publishing. The company and its founders have also been featured in *Fast Company*, *The Next Web*, and various other media.

or less—*that's* when the conversation starts to become real. Prototyping forces innovators to become super clear on what their product is—and the second you have a prototype, you can show it to potential customers and partners, and start moving forward.

Building mock web sites is just one way of prototyping ideas. As IDEO and others have demonstrated, once you get creative, there are few ideas for which you can't find a rapid, inexpensive test. The story of E-850 that we shared in the previous chapter is also a good example. When the DSM team decided that it wanted to experiment with open innovation, it didn't buy a fancy new IT system; all it did was to create a PowerPoint and put it online. Similarly, how can you make people test and prototype their ideas? Can you help them come up with simple, low-risk experiments, not only to help them learn, but also to keep them from making costly mistakes later?* (See the box, "Carlsberg's Beer Crate Implementation.")

Use Criticism: Beyond the Feel-Good Fallacy

Besides prototyping and other forms of real-world testing, a second, important tool is to expose people's ideas to frequent, critical feedback. While criticism may have a bad name, research into ideation has shown that it is crucial: teams that are told to avoid criticism will *feel* better about their ideas, but

---

*One good read on experimentation is Peter Sims, *Little Bets: How Breakthrough Ideas Emerge from Small Discoveries* (New York: Free Press, 2011), which provides numerous examples of how companies have achieved big breakthroughs through the deliberate use of small, inexpensive tests.

Carlsberg's Beer Crate Implementation

Some years ago, the major beer brewery Carlsberg decided to redesign the bottle and crate of one of its popular products, the Carlsberg Pilsner. Aimed at the Danish market, the new design would update the brand, giving it a fresher and more modern look, and would also align the local packaging with the design that Carlsberg used in other countries.

However, as the company rolled out the new design, it was blindsided by a very low-tech problem: storage space. In bars and nightclubs across the country, the bar owners had built custom-fit storage spaces for Carlsberg's beer crates, so their bartenders would have easy access to the popular beer. Unfortunately, *the new beer crates didn't fit into that space,* and since nobody had prototyped the new crate design in those settings, Carlsberg only realized the mistake *after* the countrywide launch.

In combination with other factors, the storage issue made sales go down like a bad tequila shot, and within a few months, unit sales of the Carlsberg Pilsner had fallen by 25 percent. Carlsberg eventually dropped the new design, reintroduced the old bottle and crate, and gracefully owned up to the failure by offering its customers a free *kvajebajer*, a Danish idiom best translated as "we screwed up beer." The failed launch is now a legend within the company, and to this day, people in Carlsberg still use the term "beer crate implementation" when somebody forgets to do a reality check on ideas before launching them.

they will also have worse ideas compared to teams that are allowed to be critical.

To some, this suggestion is counterintuitive. When you work in innovation, you will occasionally encounter proponents of what we call the *feel-good fallacy*. At its most extreme, this fallacy dictates that innovation must at all times be a fun, positive, and generally life-affirming experience; fun and games feature prominently, whereas criticism and confrontation are seen as creativity killers. It is especially popular in companies that see innovation as something that should energize people, implicitly, because people's regular work fails to do so.

The temptation to avoid negative emotions is superficially attractive, but ultimately wrongheaded. The reality is that innovation can be personally rewarding in many ways, but a daylong feel-good joyride it is not. Quite the contrary, every successful innovation project we have been involved in has featured not just fun, but also criticism, confrontation, frustration, and occasional verbal fights. Those aspects of the process are not pleasant, and you can work on *ameliorating* them, but it is a big mistake to avoid them entirely. The important thing is to find ways of allowing criticism into the process, not as a stopping point, but as one of several tools that can help improve the ideas.

Engineering Useful Criticism: Pixar's Approach

To witness one example of the structured use of feedback to tweak ideas, consider Pixar, a company whose near-immaculate ability to churn out blockbuster hits has made it a darling of Hollywood and innovation experts alike.

As Pixar's president Ed Catmull described in an illuminating article on the company's work routines, one of the secrets of its success is its policy of creating an environment where people get honest feedback from each other. One example is the so-called "dailies," a review process where everybody shows what he or she is working on every day, irrespective of how polished it is. By using this forcing function, Pixar avoids having its people invest time and effort in something that's not moving in the right direction.*

However, regular feedback is not enough. One of Pixar's core philosophies about choice architecture reveals itself in the "brain trust," a group of people pulled together to offer feedback when the director of a movie needs help. The critical element of the brain trust, according to Catmull, is that it is *not* a democratic process. Quite the contrary, Pixar makes it very clear that the director is in charge. Catmull explains:

> After a session, it's up to the director of the movie and his or her team to decide what to do with the advice; there are no mandatory notes, and the brain trust has no authority. This dynamic is crucial. It liberates the trust members, so they can give their unvarnished expert opinions, and it liberates the director to seek help and fully consider the advice. It took us a while to learn this. When we tried to export the brain trust model to our technical area,

---

*Frequent feedback also has another benefit. As research by Teresa Amabile and Steven Kramer has shown, the daily sense of making progress that comes from such reviews can be greatly motivating in itself, no matter how small the forward steps. See their book, *The Progress Principle: Using Small Wins to Ignite Joy, Engagement, and Creativity at Work* (Boston: Harvard Business Review Press, 2011), for more on this.

we found at first that it didn't work. Eventually, I realized why: We had given these other review groups some authority. As soon as we said, "This is purely peers giving feedback to each other," the dynamic changed, and the effectiveness of the review sessions dramatically improved.

In our experience, Pixar's approach is the key to making criticism useful. First, you should make it a regular (if not necessarily daily) event to have people share their unfinished ideas, so that the act of giving and receiving feedback becomes a relaxed, uneventful occurrence instead of a rare, high-stakes drama. Second, to the furthest extent possible, you should give people *ownership* of their ideas and make clear to everybody that the feedback process is not about making joint decisions but, rather, about helping the lead person make better decisions. Prehype's Henrik Werdelin describes the dangers of trying to tweak ideas democratically: "We have found that being *consistent* in the creation of a new product is more important than the quality of each individual sub-decision. If you try to micro-optimize every little decision that goes into shaping a new product or service, you end up with a product that points in eight different directions and makes nobody excited. It's much better to have a unified vision driving all the decisions, and then use testing and prototyping to fix the small errors as you go along." (See the box, "Make Sure Your Testing Is Real.")

Make Sure Your Testing Is Real

In January 2009, Tropicana decided to give a face lift to its well-known juice line, Tropicana Pure Premium. Among other changes, it decided to drop the iconic orange-with-a-straw image, opting instead for a design that many people felt looked like a white-label store brand.

The market reaction to the new design was not exactly favorable, to say the least. Immediately after the launch, in a stable market, unit sales of the new Tropicana line dropped by 20 percent over the span of one and a half months. As a result, the company brought back the old design in February 2009, possibly making it the fastest packaging-design reversal in modern history.

Given that result, it is tempting to think that Tropicana didn't test its new design prior to launch. However, that is not the case. Since Coca-Cola's catastrophic launch of New Coke, the soft drinks industry has not been prone to do major relaunches without prior testing, and according to PepsiCo, Tropicana's parent company, it had tested the new design with consumers prior to the launch.

PepsiCo has not shared the details of that testing process, so unfortunately we don't know the full story. However, it is probably safe to say that if your test fails to anticipate an immediate 20 percent drop in sales, you may want to take a second look at that testing process and ask if it really tests the idea as well as it should. As an innovation architect, you must make sure that tests are real and don't exist just so people can "check the box" of testing.

The risk of having people go easy on testing is also reinforced if you don't test regularly throughout the process. The second you treat testing not as a development tool, but only as a make-it-or-break-it event at the end of the process, you increase the risk that people will try to game the process, or that they unwittingly will influence the test so they get the results they want.

Framing or Testing: What to Prioritize?

In this chapter, we have covered two ways to have people tweak their ideas, namely, reframing the problem and testing the solution. The two methods should be used interchangeably, so the concurrent tweaking of the problem and the solution can feed into each other.

Depending on the nature of the idea, people may want to give more weight to one or the other. For instance, if the idea lends itself to cheap, safe prototyping, then it can be entirely appropriate to focus mostly on a trial-and-error driven, fail-forward process. On the other hand, some types of innovations are less forgiving of blind stabs in the dark. If you are dealing with the kind of idea where testing is difficult or risky, or where changes are hard to reverse, then it can make sense to have people reframe in depth before they start implementing anything. As we like to say: the famous ready-fire-aim approach works less well if you have only one shot at getting it right.

Conclusion: Suggested Action Items

- Push people to test their ideas in the real world as soon as possible, using prototypes, mock-ups, and cheap experiments. Make physical prototypes, not PowerPoints, the center of discussion in meetings.

- Create simple mechanisms or forcing functions that ensure the testing happens properly; for instance, make a rule that people can't get additional funding until they can show a video clip of their testing.

- Use the jobs-to-be-done framework to uncover all relevant aspects of consumer needs.

- Have people reframe the problem systematically. Create simple tools and processes that aid in reframing, such as forms that distinguish between problems and solutions.

- Establish a routine of people sharing unfinished ideas on an ongoing basis, making it a low-tension event rather than a dramatic finale. For instance, incorporate the idea-sharing session into an existing practice, such as weekly status meetings. Allow criticism, but make it clear that the feedback is just that; the person who owns a given idea is not obliged to incorporate the feedback, only to listen to it.

CHAPTER 5

SELECT

HOW TO MAKE PEOPLE BETTER GATEKEEPERS

MOST IDEAS ARE BAD IDEAS

Leaders must help gatekeepers get better at judging
and filtering new ideas

Johann Klein, a medical professor and future innovator, was in the business of managing hospitals, and at age thirty-four, he had become very good at his job. He was so good at it, in fact, that in 1822, despite his relatively young age, Klein was given the prestigious post of hospital director, presiding over the two maternity wards of the evocatively named *Wien Allgemeine Krankenhaus*—the Vienna General Hospital in Austria. As he took over, Klein launched a series of daring improvements that would eventually be copied by hospitals all over the world, gaining him a reputation as a first-rate medical innovator. In the two decades that followed, under Klein's able direction, the Vienna General Hospital became one of the world's leading medical institutions, drawing talented young doctors from near and far.

Today, however, Klein's contributions are largely forgotten, and if he is mentioned at all, it is not as an innovator, but as an innovation *antibody*. Because, by 1847, a young Hungarian immigrant named Ignaz Fülop Semmelweis, who was on Klein's staff, had some very unusual ideas. At the time, a mysterious disease called childbed fever was claiming the lives of the new mothers in the ward every day, sometimes killing their newborn babies as well. Nobody knew the cause of the disease; the general consensus of the medical community was that childbed fever was basically unpreventable and therefore not worth looking into.

Semmelweis thought differently. He had noticed that one of the two maternity wards at the hospital had a much higher fatality rate than the other, and by doing painstaking experiments, he managed to identify the problem. The maternity ward that was not struck by childbed fever was a nurses-only unit, whereas the other maternity ward—a ward so lethal that pregnant women would beg the doctors not to send them there—was also frequented by male medical students, who would often go directly from dissecting corpses to examining patients. Through his work, Semmelweis became the first person to discover the existence of disease-carrying germs. By implementing a strict regime of hand washing using a lime solution, Semmelweis single-handedly eradicated childbed disease from the ward practically overnight.

Selecting Ideas: When Gatekeepers Make Bad Judgments

That, unfortunately, was not the end of the story. If great ideas needed only to be *found* in order to be useful, Semmelweis's tale would have been a happy one. But to be widely implemented, ideas also need to be recognized by other people, not just the inventor. That's where Johann Klein earned his dubious legacy as the father of all innovation antibodies, because he summarily rejected Semmelweis's idea. Despite being presented with data that Semmelweis had carefully gathered, Klein refused to implement hand washing at the rest of the hospital. When Semmelweis's contract came up for renewal, Klein decided to get rid of him, giving his job to a younger, less troublesome doctor, Carl Braun. Shortly after taking over, Braun published, to much collegial acclaim, a scientific article in which he listed no fewer than thirty different causes of childbed fever, including chilliness, bad diets, and the state of being pregnant itself. Semmelweis's explanation—contact with cadaveric material—was number twenty-eight on the list. It would remain in that position until 1867, when a paper by British doctor Joseph Lister conclusively established the importance of antiseptics, ushering in a new age in medicine and restoring Semmelweis's legacy as swiftly as it destroyed Klein's. But for a lot of people, that realization came far, far too late.

Better Antibodies: The Importance of Good Gatekeeping

If you have attended an innovation conference or two, you are likely to have heard wistful speculations about how much better things would be if "we could only get rid of all the corporate innovation antibodies." If you are a young firebrand who just had one of your ideas killed, that is, of course, an appealing idea.*

But the antibody metaphor is strangely appropriate, because having antibodies is a *good* thing, not a bad thing. The vast majority of ideas are bad, and just as the human immune system keeps us healthy by attacking foreign germs, corporate gatekeepers serve the very important function of killing off bad ideas before they can invade the organization. It *is* true that internal gatekeepers sometimes kill good ideas for bad reasons, as happened to Semmelweis's insight. But the way to meet that challenge is not to remove the antibodies; it is to focus on making them *better*.

In this chapter, we focus on how you can make idea gatekeepers better at the fourth keystone behavior, that of *selecting* ideas. We use the term *gatekeeping* to distinguish it from the evaluation of ideas that happens *within* the innovation team. Innovators constantly evaluate and discard ideas as they work on implementing a new project, and much of our advice in this book—have people focus, help them connect to customers, and have them test their ideas—are really ways of arming your employees with more knowledge, so they can make good judgment calls *on their own* about where and how to invest their limited resources.

Sooner or later, though, ideas have to be evaluated by people who are *not* directly involved in the process of implementing them, that is, people who act as gatekeepers. As an innovation architect, your job is to create an environment where these gatekeepers—people like Johann Klein in our example—will make good judgment calls about the ideas that bubble up from

---

*Which brings to mind Shakespeare's immortal prescription for a better society, from his play *Henry the Sixth*: "The first thing we do, let's kill all the lawyers."

the organization, supporting the good ideas while ruthlessly killing off the bad ones.*

Four Ways to Improve Idea Selection

Fortunately, the R&D community has given the challenge of idea filtering a lot of attention. Much of the advice we share here comes from research into new product development, in which people like Robert G. Cooper and others have helped R&D managers create better idea-evaluation systems, often in the form of the so-called stage-gate processes. The challenge for innovation architects is to apply that knowledge in regular, daily management, because there people typically approach the task of evaluating new ideas more haphazardly. In a global survey in 2011, for instance, Jay Jamrog from the Institute for Corporate Productivity found that 44.9 percent of the respondents did not have *any* kind of systematic approach to idea filtering.**

In this chapter, we share four key strategies for making the gatekeepers in your business better at judging ideas:

1. Manage the decision environment

2. Determine who the best judges are

---

*Notably, gatekeepers need not be part of any formal review board; in your business, whoever takes part in evaluating new ideas on a regular basis effectively works as a gatekeeper, whether this is formally acknowledged or not. The advice we share here applies equally whether you have a formal process, or whether your gatekeeping happens informally, as a natural part of the work flow.

**Jay Jamrog, *Innovate or Perish: Building a Culture of Innovation*, Institute for Corporate Productivity, 2011. An older survey by the same author found that in 2005, the number was 48 percent, making for a rather modest improvement of three percent in six years.

3. Review the evaluation criteria

4. Calibrate the process regularly

1. Manage the Decision Environment, not the Individual Decisions

As we have stated in previous chapters, when you try to help people innovate, the key is not to change who they are, but to change the environment they work in, creating the conditions for innovative behavior. This applies to gatekeepers as well. When trying to improve people's ability to filter ideas, the first thing you should look at is the decision environment of the gatekeepers: are the overall process and setting appropriate for the task? To illustrate, we share the experience of an innovation architect in action, showing how he works to improve the decision making in his company.

An Innovation Architect at Work: David Rimer at Index Ventures

If you are looking for expert practitioners in the art of idea filtering, talk to people who are venture capitalists (VCs). As early-stage investors in start-ups, VCs spend huge amounts of time evaluating business ideas, and a significant part of their success depends on their ability to pick the few potential winners from a vast river of incoming projects. Most VCs review and reject hundreds of business plans for every one they decide to invest in.

The Geneva-based VC firm Index Ventures has been particularly good at this sport. Founded in 1996, Index Ventures has been an early-stage investor in Skype and other big successes, and in terms of financial performance, the forty-five-person company generally ranks in the top 10 percent of the US venture capital industry. Some of its most successful bets have earned Index (and its financial backers) a return of up to forty times the invested amount. Among its more recent investments are start-ups that will sound familiar to creative cognoscenti: Flipboard, Path, SoundCloud, MOO, BetFair, LoveFilm, Dropbox, and even Moleskine, the company that proved you could turn a supreme commodity like paper notebooks into a high-priced best seller.

One of the secrets behind Index's success is the highly methodical approach it takes to *engineering the decision environment* around the evaluation process, personified in the work of David Rimer, the company's operating partner and de facto innovation architect. In your average VC firm, the partners all tend to be deal makers, whereas nonpartners mostly staff the operational roles. But as Rimer told us, when he and his partners shaped Index, they took a different approach: "We believe that operations is too critical to be treated as a mere sideshow to the deal making, so I have taken the role of Operating Partner to make sure it receives the focus it needs. As part of this, I constantly engineer, tweak and evaluate the way we make decisions, so my partners and I have the best possible chances of making good judgment calls."

One example is the so-called *exit* decision, meaning the VC's decision of whether or not to sell its stake in a current investment. If, for instance, a promising start-up that Index has shares in goes public, Rimer and his fellow partners have to evaluate the potential of their start-up: has this company gone as far and as high as we can take it? Given the offer at hand, should we exit the investment now? Or do we believe we can get a higher price if we hold on to our shares for a while longer? Holding on to the investment can be the difference between doubling your investment and doubling it by five—or it can be the difference between doubling it and *halving* it, in case the start-up subsequently stumbles.

As Rimer examined Index's track record, he noticed a clear trend: Index tended to exit its investments *too late*. Several times, Index had held on to public shares, turned down great offers for its shares in a company, or, in certain cases, had opposed M&A offers for its companies, only to see the value of the investment subsequently fall. That happens to all venture capital firms, but in Index's case, there were just too many instances and not a lot of cases of premature exits. As Rimer looked into this, he identified the issue:

> The problem was related to the decision-making process. For each company we invest in, one of our partners becomes the "lead" partner—typically the one who discovered the company—and normally, that person has the final say on all matters related to the investment. That tends to work well because the lead partner is the one who best understands the business. But when it came to the exit decision, I found that the lead partners were systematically overoptimistic. Having discovered the idea and nurtured the team to success, they would tend to fall in love with the company—and as a result, they tended to think that the future potential was greater than an objective look at the facts might warrant.

Building the Architecture of Idea Filtering

To improve the quality of judgment calls, Rimer started changing the process for exit decisions:

> I tried different approaches, and not all of them worked. For instance, we played with making outsiders part of the voting process, by pulling in someone we trusted from outside Index. But that didn't work out; among other things, the outsiders didn't have any skin in the game, which biased their decisions in a bad way. So we stopped that and tried something else until we found a good model. Now, we have a dedicated committee involved in all the exits— and while the lead partner is involved with that team, he only has a minority vote.

The lesson from Rimer's story is not about the particulars of how Index engineers its decision environment; for your business, the best way to do it may be different. Rather, Rimer's story highlights the overall approach innovation architects must take, analyzing, tweaking, and improving the gatekeeping process.

- Study the gatekeeping function in your business. Does it kill too few or too many ideas? Are the gatekeepers biased toward overly low-risk (or high-risk) ideas?

- Look at how other business units (or competitors) handle idea filtering. Are there other units in your organization that do a good job? What is different about their approach?

- Experiment with making changes to the gatekeeping process. For instance, can you run two different gate-keeping processes in parallel, experimenting to see if a different approach could work better?

There are few limits to what kind of tweaking you can do to engineer a better decision environment, and some of them can be surprising. For instance, sometimes it makes sense to *blind* gatekeepers to part of the process. The research of Claudia Goldin and Cecilia Rouse provides a memorable example, as it demonstrated that classical orchestras suffered from a bias against hiring female musicians. Simply put, the auditions were run by men who believed, openly or otherwise, that women were simply inferior musicians, with the result that some of the orchestras had only one or two women in them. However, when the orchestras made a simple change to the audition process, the hiring of women increased: the orchestras set up a screen and carpeted the floors, so the judges couldn't see the gender of the player or divine it from the clicking of high-heeled shoes on hardwood floors.

Similarly, businesses may also benefit from selectively blinding their gatekeepers. For instance, from his experience running idea management systems in multiple companies, former CEO of Imaginatik, Mark Turrell, found that anonymous ideas are three times as likely to deliver results, compared to nonanonymous ideas. The anonymity allows people to submit good but politically sensitive ideas, and it also prevents gate-keepers from discarding good ideas that come from people they dislike, as Klein did in the case of Semmelweis. What changes could *you* make to the architecture of idea filtering? (See the box, "Have a Separate Pipeline for Game-Changing Ideas.")

Have a Separate Pipeline for Game-Changing Ideas

The approach we describe is primarily aimed at creating what Clay Christensen calls *sustaining* innovations, that is, ideas that help sustain and grow the current business, as opposed to disruptive innovation, which tends to reconfigure or even destroy the way industries work. In relation to gatekeeping, the problem with such game-changing ideas is that they tend to disrupt not only the market, but also the internal way of operating, and that makes it likely that internal gatekeepers will either kill them or turn them into more incremental ideas.

A widely used way to deal with this issue is to have separate pipelines for the two kinds of ideas, giving the more disruptive ideas a chance to bypass the regular local gatekeepers and their (rightful) bias toward less disruptive ideas. This means that, as an innovation architect, you must figure out if your company has such a pipeline or escape hatch for disruptive ideas, and if your people know it is there. In case you don't have a pipeline for disruptive ideas, creating one can be very simple. In many companies, it is accepted practice for people with game-changing ideas to simply send an e-mail directly to the CEO.* While it may be outside your power to implement a game-changing idea within your own business unit, you can at least make sure it survives to be evaluated by higher powers.

---

*Incidentally, this low-tech approach is a solution that predates e-mail. In their great book, *Winning Though Innovation*, Michael Tushman and Charles O'Reilly describe how in 1898, the US Navy implemented a new, superior technology only because a young officer, after exhausting all other channels, sent his idea directly to US President Theodore Roosevelt.

2. Determine Who the Best Judges Are

A crucial element of any selection process is *who* does the filtering? The composition of the gatekeepers tends to affect the quality and nature of the outcome as much as the procedures they follow. In a large-scale survey published in 2011, researchers at the Institute for Corporate Productivity looked into how different companies approach the idea-filtering process (see table 5-1).

As the survey made clear, there is no dominant approach to idea filtering, unless you count not having a policy as a deliberate approach. The key thing, when determining who the judges should be, is to be mindful of the various *positional* biases that people bring to the table. For instance, if you consider the approaches in light of the Semmelweis story, you will see that

TABLE 5-1

Most popular methods for evaluating ideas

Most popular methods for evaluating ideas	All respondents
There is no standard policy for reviewing and evaluating ideas	44.9%
There are several different ways a new idea can be reviewed and evaluated	27.4%
Within the organization, there is an independent review and evaluation process for ideas	8.7%
Ideas are reviewed and evaluated by the unit manager in the location where the idea was proposed	7.2%
The employee is responsible for starting and managing the review process	5.2%
Ideas are reviewed and evaluated by the unit that would be impacted the most by the idea	4.8%
Other	1.8%

Source: Based on Jay Jamrog, *Innovate or Perish: Building a Culture of Innovation* (Institute for Corporate Productivity, 2011).

the various kinds of gatekeepers will bring both good and bad factors into play.

The direct boss. Having someone's immediate superior evaluate her ideas carries the great advantage of being expedient and easy to do; in organizations that don't have a policy for filtering ideas, it is probably the de facto standard. But direct managers can be biased in various ways. In Klein's case, if Semmelweis's idea were true, it would have cast a bad light on Klein, because the practice of letting medical students dissect corpses was one of Klein's own innovations and an important pillar of his success. Klein could not possibly have predicted the consequences of his own innovation, but it could still have destroyed his reputation, making it more than likely that Klein was negatively disposed against Semmelweis's idea, unconsciously and perhaps consciously as well. Also, research by Tanya Menon and Jeffrey Pfeffer suggests that as individuals, managers are often biased against using internal ideas, among other reasons, because learning from their own people confers less status on the managers, compared to sourcing new ideas from the outside.

The affected unit. Letting the affected party judge the idea makes intuitive sense, but it also carries the risk of having a good idea killed because it goes counter to local incentives. In Semmelweis's case, many of the other doctors on his ward resisted the practice of hand washing, less for theoretical reasons than for the sheer inconvenience of having to constantly wash their hands with lime solution. (Even today, hand washing remains an unpopular activity with doctors, and the infection rate from germs carried by hospital staff is significant.)

Such local incentives aren't just about convenience; they can be an entirely sensible way the business works. In the alcoholic beverages company Diageo, for instance, the managers of the vodka brand Smirnoff resisted the introduction of Smirnoff Ice, a mixer product that threatened to cannibalize its sales of regular Smirnoff (and thereby dig into their personal bonuses). Had Diageo allowed the Smirnoff managers to determine the fate of Smirnoff Ice, chances are it would not have seen the light of day, much less the crepuscular gloom of bars and night-clubs. The company introduced the product anyway and ended up creating a new, successful category in the hard-to-penetrate liquor market.

> An independent review. An independent review board is capable of judging an idea with more objectivity: assuming that the board is composed of multiple people from different backgrounds, the influence from individual or positional biases is mitigated. However, sometimes you *need* subjectivity, meaning firsthand knowledge of the relevant domain. Independent review boards often lack *personal immersion* in and firsthand knowledge of the domain that the idea involves, making them more likely to make bad or uninformed judgment calls, or favor ambitious but unfeasible ideas over less ambitious but more actionable ideas. In the case of Klein, Semmelweis wrote letters to several prominent European doctors describing his idea, but because

these doctors, unlike Klein, could not *see* Semmelweis's work firsthand, they had little information to base their decision on, besides Semmelweis's poor reputation.*

Getting the Right Mix

As these examples highlight, there is rarely one right answer in deciding who makes the judgment call on new ideas; each party will bring different biases into the picture. Nonetheless, a few pieces of advice can improve the gatekeeping process:

- **Involve several people with different biases.** A simple way to ameliorate various biases is to make sure that more than one person judges the ideas, circulating the idea widely before it is judged. This doesn't necessarily mean you should make the process democratic; there is nothing wrong with having a single person making the decisions, as long as that person does not make them in isolation, but is informed by other opinions. Even if a good idea is killed this way, the circulation makes it possible for people in other areas to pursue it.

- **Try using alternative decision makers.** Managers are not always the best decision makers. Can you experiment with having other groups decide or at least giving them a strong voice in the process? Google, for instance, puts heavy emphasis on how many colleagues a programmer

---

*The problem with Semmelweis's idea was that it went against the reigning medical theory at the time, which posited that diseases were caused by bad miasmas and imbalances of the four bodily humors. It is therefore likely that the *only* way one of these experts could have been convinced was to witness the effect of hand washing directly.

can recruit to work on an idea, and also involves the public through its Google Labs initiative, letting the market test some of its ideas. Kickstarter, a web site that helps people with ideas find investors, simply uses crowd funding to determine which ideas get support. Can you test to see if the gatekeeping process should be outsourced, partially or entirely?

- Have gatekeepers experience the idea firsthand. Some ideas don't come across well in a PowerPoint slide and are at risk of getting killed if independent reviewers who don't have experience with the relevant domain judge them. A partial remedy is to let the gatekeepers *experience* the idea personally, instead of just evaluating it based on a presentation. As we discuss in chapter 6, on stealthstorming, there are many ways of creating a demo or prototype of a new idea. If you make such "immersed" idea testing a standard part of the gatekeeping process, you decrease the risk that it kills good ideas that happen to be hard to convey on paper.*

3. Review the Evaluation Criteria

When looking at the *criteria* gatekeepers use to evaluate ideas, an innovation architect should first ask: do the criteria fit the overall strategic aims of the business? Gatekeepers may be using criteria that are not in fact aligned with what the business is trying to achieve.

---

*Eric von Hippel calls this "sticky information"—that is, knowledge that is hard to convey to others, especially people who aren't in the same situation or physical location. See Eric von Hippel, "'Sticky Information' and the Locus of Problem Solving: Implications for Innovation," *Management Science* 40, no. 4 (April 1994).

Are the Criteria in Line with the Strategy?

General Motors was long considered one of America's bright and shining beacons of industry. In a *New York Times* article from 2008, journalist Micheline Maynard described how, over the last few decades, General Motors had come up with several new and potentially game-changing ideas long before its competitors saw them. In the 1980s, GM spotted the potential for small cars, a market that was just beginning to surface, and invested money in developing small-car prototypes under the Saturn brand. In the 1990s, far ahead of its competitors, employees at GM invented the EV1 electric car, an early precursor to the hybrid cars now on the market. None of these potential game changers made it to market, because again and again, when it was time to double down on the innovative ideas and bring them to market, the gatekeepers inside General Motors chose to kill the projects.

The reason? The people in charge of investment decisions were utterly focused on short-term results and consistently prioritized projects that would bring in cash quickly and predictably. This meant that the more radical ideas—which almost always have longer investment horizons and are much harder to evaluate—were consistently killed off in favor of smaller ideas, such as introducing a known car model in a new color or with a new feature.

The result will not surprise students of the history of innovation: the steadfast refusal to finance long-term innovation meant that GM was repeatedly overtaken by more forward-looking competitors. When the market for minivans grew big in the 1980s, the majority of sales went to Chrysler, despite the fact that the idea of a minivan had circulated within General Motors for more than a decade. In the early 1990s, when the market for SUVs surfaced, it was Ford and Chrysler that introduced them, with GM taking an additional five years to enter the market. And for hybrid cars, perhaps the most powerful illustration of GM's filtering problem, Toyota brought its Prius hybrid model to the US market in 2000 and has since sold more than 2.5 million cars. General Motors—which had experimented with hybrid technology since the 1970s—didn't launch its Volt hybrid until 2010, a decade after Toyota.

Are There Too Many Criteria?

Evaluation processes, like mushrooms and moustaches, can grow wild if left unchecked. As gatekeepers start drawing up their checklists, they often take pride in being comprehensive and making sure that they have covered all possible angles. However, while having too few criteria can invalidate the process, there is also a danger in having too *many* criteria.

At a German company, we sat in on a presentation where the executive in charge of innovation explained how the filtering system worked. He needed several dozen PowerPoint slides to explain the system, an elaborate process in which ideas were graded on a very large number of criteria, applied at different stages by multiple gatekeepers. The executives who witnessed the presentation with us didn't question this; on the contrary, they expressed their approval of the system's thoroughness. Indeed, the system worked well in the sense that it protected the company from foolish mistakes; any idea that made it through the filter was fairly certain to be a safe bet. It worked so well, in fact, that when we asked the managers, none could mention an example of a mistake that had gotten past the review process. The problem, of course, was that the approved ideas were also certain to be utterly incremental, because the only types of ideas that scored highly on that many criteria were those that were most obvious. More radical ideas scored very poorly on the many criteria where the answer was either unknown, uncertain, or below some threshold value.

Similarly, you should ask the gatekeepers whether the criteria could benefit from being shaved down to the essentials. Are there factors to remove? Are there too many? Are they simple to understand and to apply?

4. Calibrate the Process Regularly

In addition to considering biases and selection criteria, it is important to consider the incentives of the gatekeepers in the gatekeeping process itself. For instance, a manager we know was responsible for tending the company's idea pipeline, gathering suggestions from the employees, and taking the good ones to the next level. In this case, her boss measured the team's performance on one key criterion: the percentage of received ideas that were implemented. The manager told us she was struggling with how to implement *more* ideas, so she could reach her goal of taking at least 5 percent of the incoming ideas to the next level.

This metric, of course, will tell you if the good folks in the innovation department are busy at work, or if they are just goofing around while the suggestion boxes go untended. But when you consider the cardinal rule of this chapter—*most ideas are bad ideas*—the problem becomes apparent. Assuming all your employees decide to binge on bad whiskey tomorrow and then stuff two thousand really horrible ideas into the suggestion boxes, this evaluation criterion forces the team to implement one hundred horrible ideas. As part of your review of the gatekeeping process, remember to consider if the gatekeepers are measured in a way that makes sense.

Some Tips for Killing Existing Projects

A frequent problem in organizations is the difficulty of stopping ongoing projects. Some initiatives are dictated from above and can be hard to fight. But many other projects are self-initiated and *could* be stopped with a local decision, only somehow that doesn't happen, causing an unnecessary and perpetual state of project overload. How do you kill projects?

The most important rule is similar to the advice given in first-aid courses: *First, stop the accident.* If you witness a traffic accident, *before* you rush to the aid of the wounded, you have to stop the oncoming traffic so the accident doesn't get any worse. Similarly, if your organization is suffering from a plague of projects, stopping a few of them only fixes the symptoms of the plague. Your first step should be to change the way projects are *started*. One of the best tips is to make sure all projects are launched with a kill switch of some kind, that is, tangible metrics and milestones defining when the project should be put on probation and ultimately shut down.* Reframing projects as time-limited experiments can also help, so the default decision is to stop the project. Also, as we explained in the chapter on focusing, being

---

*When defining kill switches for a new project, it is a good idea to be generous—that is, if you put an expiration date on a new idea, give the team several *more* months than they think they need to prove it. Projects always take longer to implement than people think, so if you define kill switches that are too strict, the temptation to ignore them becomes bigger. It's better to set generous but "hard" kill switches—give people a full year if they say they only need six months—so when the kill switch is finally activated, it is clear to everybody that it is fair to shut down the project.

clear on the overall goals of the business can help determine whether a proposed project is off strategy before it starts.

Beyond this, a few pointers can make the process of killing projects easier and (slightly) less painful:

- **Evaluate multiple projects at once.** It's very hard to judge ongoing projects in isolation. Evaluate all ongoing projects together, if possible.

- **Make people vote for survivors.** If you give other people a vote in the decision-making process, have them vote for which projects to *save*, not which to kill. The outcome is the same, but we've found that people find it easier to be cast as project saviors instead of project executioners.

- **Bring your strategy razor.** Projects are often allowed to live too long because they are labeled strategic projects, without necessarily being particularly strategic. Being clear on the exact strategic aims of the business—and starting the review meeting by sharing them—can help decide what projects to cut.

- **Regularly schedule the reviews.** Set up a specific, fixed schedule for project reviews. If not, they tend to be postponed indefinitely.

- **Accept the pain.** Nobody likes killing projects; accept that it's painful and do it anyway. Showing unwarranted mercy won't remove the pain; it just prolongs it and distributes it over more time and people.

Who Guards the Gatekeepers?

In a *New York Times* article discussing his book on decision making, *Thinking, Fast and Slow*, Nobel Prize winner Daniel Kahneman shares an interesting story from his early career in the Israeli army. Kahneman, along with a team of psychologists, had the job of evaluating the leadership potential of candidates for officer training. To that end, they had devised a series of tests where they could see the candidates in action, solving various teamwork challenges. Based on how people performed in these scenarios, Kahneman and his colleagues felt very confident in their evaluations of the candidates.

That confidence was not justified. Kahneman's team regularly received feedback on the candidates' actual performance, and, as he wrote in the article, "the story was always the same: our ability to predict performance at the school was negligible. Our forecasts were better than blind guesses, but not by much." Yet, as Kahneman points out, the bad feedback *did not change the approach of the psychologists*. The team kept running its tests and kept believing in the evaluations. Kahneman continues: "The statistical evidence of our failure should have shaken our confidence in our judgments of particular candidates, but it did not. It should also have caused us to moderate our predictions, but it did not. We knew as a general fact that our predictions were little better than random guesses, but we continued to feel and act as if each particular prediction was valid."

The cognitive blindness that Kahneman discovered is also at work for corporate gatekeepers. With a simple but sound idea-filtering process, good selection criteria, and the right mix of people in the gatekeeping role, you increase the likelihood that people make good decisions, but you also need to verify that it actually works. You need, in brief, to monitor and calibrate both the criteria and the gatekeepers themselves, because often gatekeepers will persist with their gut feeling *even when direct evidence contradicts it*. As David Rimer did in Index Ventures, the innovation architect should periodically check up on the review process itself and evaluate whether it works. (See the box, "Some Tips for Killing Existing Projects.")

Conclusion: Suggested Action Items

- Look into the way your business evaluates ideas. Has somebody thought about how it should happen? Does it work?

- Check how the process operates. Is the mix of gatekeepers appropriate? Do they use sensible criteria? Are the criteria aligned with the overall goals? Do employees know the criteria?

- Consider if alternative evaluation processes could work. Could you experiment with letting customers evaluate ideas directly? Could you make parts of the process more democratic, for example, with some kind of crowd sorting?

- Verify that there is a separate pipeline or escape hatch for disruptive ideas, and that people know it. If need be, work with the top management to establish one.

- Check to see if anyone monitors the actual performance of the gatekeepers. If you are a gatekeeper yourself, take a hint from Kahneman's findings and rigorously apply these lessons to yourself as well (or even better, have a third party monitor your performance).

CHAPTER 6

STEALTHSTORM

HOW TO HELP PEOPLE NAVIGATE THE POLITICS OF INNOVATION

STEALTHSTORMING RULES
Leaders must help people deal with organizational politics

Many people, especially those who are creative, harbor a sound hatred for corporate politics. Secure in the conviction that a good idea should win on its own merits, some innovators neglect or even refuse to deal with the *realpolitik* of working in a big organization. That is a problem because successful innovation is as much about politics as it is about having a great idea. Dealing with corporate politics is like sailing in a strong crosswind. If people stubbornly ignore it, it will slow them down, blow them off course, or throw them onto the rocks. But if they manage to *harness* its power, it can propel them toward the finish line with extraordinary speed.

In this chapter, we show how you can help innovators deal with the politics of innovation. As the English language doesn't contain a (non-awkward) word for the multitude of behaviors that are involved in navigating organizational politics, our search for a more all-encompassing term led us to coin our own word for it, namely, *stealthstorming*.* In contrast to its more flamboyant cousin *brainstorming*, stealthstorming is meant to invoke a more subdued, under-the-radar approach to innovation: one that is compatible with the culture of a conservative organization. (Think of it as creativity in pinstripes.)

Stealthstorming: Five Aspects of Corporate Creativity

Next, we discuss five specific aspects of stealthstorming, sharing advice on how you can help people navigate the political reefs and barriers of the organization. In particular, we return repeatedly to the story of pfizerWorks, sharing some lessons in stealthstorming that Jordan Cohen learned as he built the service:

1. Connect your people to power brokers

2. Help people create a story around their idea

3. Make people demonstrate value early

---

*Language mavens may point out that the word *politicking* has an imperative form, but frankly, apart from its sheer awkwardness, we are pretty sure that if we had used *politick*, people would assume we made a spelling error.

4. Help people secure more resources

5. Help people manage their personal brand

1. Connect Your People to Power Brokers

As the sociologist Everett M. Rogers described in his seminal book *Diffusion of Innovations*, even the best of ideas can meet strong resistance when you try to make whole communities of people adopt them. Rogers put forth the historical example of scurvy, the disease that killed an estimated 2 million sailors due to vitamin C deficiency. As we know from the diaries of famous British sea captains like Francis Drake, the cure for scurvy, fresh citrus fruit, was already known in the late 1590s, but it wasn't until 1795, around two hundred years later, that the British Admiralty finally made it standard policy to bring citrus juice on long voyages.

Many have cited the story of scurvy as an example of how slow societies can be to adopt new ideas. But there is an interesting element to the story that most people don't question: namely, *why did the policy become standard in 1795?* As we saw in the previous chapter, the medical establishment was still in the grip of bad theories half a century later, when Semmelweis tried and failed to introduce hand washing. So what made the British Admiralty see the light in 1795?

When Life Hands You Lemons . . .

As it turns out, the decision was not a matter of gradual bottom-up adoption. In his book *Scurvy*, the Canadian historian Stephen R. Bown explains that it was in fact due to the actions of one man, namely, the estimable First Baronet Gilbert

Blane of Blanefield. Before Blane entered the picture, several other doctors, using reams of evidence, had already tried and failed to make the Admiralty mandate the use of citrus fruits. What made Blane different was his political capital: he was neither a sailor nor a trained surgeon, but he hailed from a wealthy and respected Scottish family, and he had used that social springboard to gain the favor of influential men and build a great career for himself. An eager networker and an eminent social climber, Blane was apparently not the most sympathetic of characters. As Bown puts it, while he was great at flattering his betters: "Blane was called Chilblain behind his back because of his distant and chilly behavior towards those he considered his social inferiors." However, Blane had read a treatise by the surgeon James Lind recommending citrus fruits, and after making a seafaring friend test Lind's cure, he became convinced that it worked. Thus, in 1795, as Blane was appointed to the navy's Sick and Hurt Board, he quickly used his political talents to make it standard policy in the entire navy.

In other words, we owe the defeat of scurvy to a snob with a penchant for schmoozing. But as another naval doctor would later put it, cited in Bown's book, "there is no need to be critical of Blane and condemn him as a snob. Thank God he was, if it meant that he had the power of using cajolery and flattery to get his own way with the powers that be . . . Without Blane's popularity with [his boss] and the rulers of the King's Navy, the country might have had to wait even more than 40 years [for the cure to be implemented]."

Jordan Cohen and David Kreutter Revisited

If you want to gain support for a good idea, few things are more helpful than powerful friends. Fortunately, while it takes political flair to reach the upper echelons of power, not all corporate superiors share Blane's chilly downward disposition. Once you manage to convince a senior executive to believe in an idea—and notably, in the people who will carry it out—all manner of things political will start to become easier.

As mentioned in chapter 1, one such sponsor played a critical role in the creation of pfizerWorks. Initially, Jordan Cohen's primary sponsor was his immediate boss, Bob Orr, who supported Cohen's extracurricular activities and believed in the nascent potential of the idea. But the idea really started taking off the minute Cohen gained the support of David Kreutter.

As we explained earlier, Kreutter initially helped Cohen by giving advice, pulling some strings, and helping him navigate among the different stakeholders. But later on, when it was time to find a proper organizational home for pfizerWorks, the connection to Kreutter proved invaluable. Kreutter explains:

pfizerWorks was originally part of a group called Global Operations, but this was not the ideal home for the project. Global Operations deals with real estate, facilities management and similar issues that had little in common with what Jordan was doing. And from a financial perspective, Jordan's budget was relatively small for a unit that dealt with near-billion-dollar budgets, meaning that pfizerWorks would never get the amount of attention that it needed as a start-up operation.

One option we discussed was the Procurement division, whose activities were more aligned with what Jordan was doing. But I think the relationship would have become somewhat transactional in nature, focused on cost savings, minimizing expenditure, and so on—and pfizerWorks, in both Jordan's and my mind, had a greater potential than that. pfizerWorks was a strong potential vehicle for driving change and productivity; it shouldn't be run as just another cost center. So in the end, Jordan and I worked together to shift pfizerWorks over to my own business unit, U.S. Commercial Operations, where we could give it the attention and the resources it required.*

As is apparent from the story, there are many hidden subtleties in making corporate innovations happen, and without someone who understands the complex dynamics of a company's governance structures, it becomes very easy to make bad choices. For this reason, you must help people establish a similar network of sponsors and advisers.

Here are some tips for connecting people to sponsors:

- Work with people to identify potential senior sponsors in their personal networks, for example, former bosses from other departments. Check your own network as well, but remember that it works best if the innovators themselves already have a personal history of trust with the sponsor.

---

*Personal conversation with David Kreutter, August 2009. Finding the right organizational home for pfizerWorks later proved to be crucially important, as Cohen eventually left Pfizer to lead the knowledge worker productivity practice at PA Consulting, assisting others in increasing organizational productivity. In other cases, the departure of the original innovator might have meant the end of the project. But because Cohen, with Kreutter's help, had engineered a strong architecture around the initiative, vesting it in the systems instead of in himself, pfizerWorks didn't end with his departure. Quite the contrary, at the time of writing, pfizerWorks is headed by Tanya Carr-Waldron and continues to grow and be very popular with Pfizer's employees.

- Before reaching out, have your people clarify *why their innovation is interesting* to each sponsor, considering its value from their vantage points. Ask them to consider if there are any reasons for the sponsor to *oppose* the idea (in which case, they may want to stay off that person's radar).

- As they establish the connection, emphasize its *informal nature*, and instruct your people to *ask only for advice and opinions.** (Some potential sponsors may react negatively to unsolicited requests for support in the first meetings, whereas almost everybody reacts positively to requests for advice.)

- *Push people to find sponsors early in the process.* Advice is most valuable in the beginning, and the sponsor will likely get more involved if she feels she is part of shaping the idea, as opposed to being sold on a finished concept.

- Finally, make sure people *maintain the connections* to their key advisers as they move forward. Once people agree to become involved as advisers, they will expect to be kept in the loop.

2. Help People Create a Story Around Their Idea

To succeed, ideas ultimately need to be sold to many different stakeholders within the organization. When trying to sell their ideas, many people often make the mistake of thinking

---

*Here, as in general, we assume that you will be in the same position as Bob Orr was with regard to Cohen, that is, you won't have time to be directly involved, but will act as a facilitator and adviser to your people. In special cases, however, you might want take a more active role in the political aspects in particular.

that buying into an idea is mostly a *logical* choice. To that end, they build elaborate business cases demonstrating why their idea makes sense. Creating a solid business case is indeed necessary, but it is rarely enough to convince people. Especially in the early stages, when the innovation will be rough and undefined, buying into the idea is equally an emotional choice and a social choice. Leaders need to make people work on the *narrative* of their idea. This is where the power of storytelling comes in.

Storytelling: Have People Build a Narrative

The last time you saw a charity drive, say, for alleviating poverty in another country or providing disaster relief to a stricken nation, did the campaign use statistics or spreadsheets to convince you to donate your money? Chances are that it didn't, because through years of experience, nongovernmental organizations have learned that most people respond more to personal stories. That's why their campaigns tend to feature one specific, named individual, often a child: "For just $25 a year, you can help Miriam go to school instead of working in a factory." Christian Budtz, coauthor of the book *Storytelling* and an expert in the strategic use of narratives, comments: "The power of stories is a primal thing. Throughout most of human history, before we had books and computers and video seminars, storytelling was the primary vehicle for sharing our knowledge, and to this day, it has a deep, intuitive resonance with people. Simply put, we tend to find ideas much more convincing and memorable when they are delivered in the shape of a story."

The deliberate use of storytelling can help people sell their ideas as well. Cohen often shared the story of his employee Paul, a talented MIT graduate and a young father, and how Cohen noticed that Paul was often in the office until late in the evening because of grunt work, work that pfizerWorks could help alleviate. The founder of eBay, Pierre Omidyar, famously said he invented eBay to help his wife sell her collection of Pez dispensers, a story that he later admitted was mostly a marketing tool. In a similar vein—and preferably without taking too many creative liberties—you should help people identify a good story about their idea and then hone that story until it is well told. When your people explain what their ideas are, do they have a compelling, individual example of how it can make a difference? Is the story simple and memorable enough for other people to spread it? (See the box, "Social Proof: How *Not* to Sell Your Idea.")

3. Make People Demonstrate Value Early

In *The Little Black Book of Innovation*, Scott Anthony shares Clayton Christensen's concept of the "ticking clock," a deadline for creating results that all innovators face: "You never know quite how fast the clock is ticking, or when the alarm is set, but you can be darn sure that at some point, it will ring. The proverbial clock always strikes midnight. If that moment comes and all you have is potential, you'd better start polishing your résumé." As Anthony points out, no matter how big the long-term potential of an idea, innovators must still aim to deliver some quick wins, lest they get axed by the well-known corporate penchant for immediate gratification.

Social Proof: How *Not* to Sell Your Idea

When people consider whether or not to try a new service, the concept of *social proof* plays a huge role. As shown by Robert Cialdini and other students of influence tactics, people take strong cues from their peers, and will often do the same as they perceive the majority does. The power of social proof is why late-night TV ads tell you that "our lines may be busy," instead of "our salespeople are ready to take your call." It creates the perception that lots of other people are calling in as well, which makes for a measurable difference in the ad's efficiency.

In one company we worked with, one of its support functions tried to launch a new Internet initiative, aiming to get the employees to start using it. However, the team had failed to consider how social proof works: on the nicely designed promo posters, the team declared, "Be the first to use the new platform!" Unsurprisingly, the new service was not exactly overrun by employees eager to be the first guinea pigs.

In a telling comparison, when Cohen and his team put up posters advertising pfizerWorks internally, they took the opposite approach. The posters featured pictures of employees from the local office, with taglines like "Jane's weekend was saved by pfizerWorks." Like Cohen, make your people use social proof when they promote their ideas.

The advice is excellent. If at all possible, you must make your people follow it. However, the nature of people's ideas *may* be such that delivering quick wins is not an option. In that case, there are two good rules to remember. The first is that for the clock to strike, it first has to be *started*, and that often won't happen until people go "above the radar" with the project in some way, for example, by getting funding or otherwise attracting attention. By keeping the project in stealth mode to start with, finding ways of tweaking it that can be done within your available means, you can often postpone the moment that the clock starts ticking.

Second, the more you can make gatekeepers, sponsors, and other purse-string holders personally *believe* in the idea, not just in a results-oriented sense but also emotionally, the more tolerance they will show toward lack of immediate progress. To make them do that, something more than storytelling may be needed.

Have People Create Personal Experiences

When it comes to convincing people, the single most potent sales tool is not verbal. In *Influencer*, a book that uses the science of persuasion to discuss behavior change, Kerry Patterson and his coauthors point out an important truth: *The great persuader is personal experience*. If you want people to change their minds about an idea, often the single best thing you can do is to make them experience it themselves.

In a story described in *Influencer*, the management of a US manufacturing plant needed to sell an *unpopular* idea to its employees: that they had to change the way they worked because their Japanese competitors were up to 40 percent more effective. At first, the managers tried to convince people with hard data and PowerPoint presentations, to very little effect. The workers felt they were already working hard and simply refused to believe that their Japanese counterparts could be significantly more effective. So to convince the workers, the managers came up with a different strategy: they invited ten of the most vocal employees to visit a manufacturing plant in Japan. Once the employees saw for themselves how the Japanese teams worked, day and night, they realized that the problem was real, an effect that no amount of verbal persuasion could have achieved.

This method works with innovations as well. (Remember the feeling you got the first time you played with an iPad?) When people come up with a really good idea, both they and possibly you will come to believe in its potential, emotionally as well as rationally. That probably didn't happen just on the basis of an ROI calculation. A business case will rarely make a gatekeeper fall in love with an idea to the extent your people did, but a convincing personal experience just might do the trick. For really important sales pitches, can you have people engineer a personal experience that sells their idea? Or, if the target group is different from the gatekeepers, can you at least make them witness the impact firsthand?* (See the box, "My Daughter Hated It.")

---

*For instance, after the press conference where Lego launched its new line of programmable MindStorm bricks, it invited all of the assembled journalists and TV crews into an adjacent room where groups of children were playing happily with the new bricks. This firsthand experience likely did its part to make the journalists believe in the product (and also, it provided the TV crews with some excellent footage for the daily sunshine story that most newscasts end with).

"My Daughter Hated It"

A client asked an advertising agency for a commercial aimed at children. The team members came up with a great idea, and to build their case, they tested the ad on a group of children within the target demographic, with very positive results. The agency showed the test results to the client, who said that he liked it, but would sleep on it before making a final decision. The next day, however, the client had some bad news: he didn't think the idea would work. The agency had to come up with something different. Surprised, the team asked why he had changed his mind. The client answered, "Well, I showed the ad to my daughter yesterday evening, and she didn't like it."

People in advertising will tell you lots of similar stories: it's an unspoken truth that many advertising people consider their clients to be stupid, irrational, risk-averse, and utterly incapable of recognizing greatness. Of course, the team must have been frustrated to see their idea killed. For all they knew, the daughter might have been angry with her dad that day. But what the story really shows is this: *people put more credence in things they personally experience.* The one bad reaction from his daughter trumped the good reactions of the children in the test group, not only because she was his daughter, but also because *the client was there to see it,* whereas the reactions of the other children were conveyed to him only indirectly. If the team had convinced the client to witness the test personally, the story would likely have had a different outcome.

4. Help People Secure More Resources

Some companies have adopted the practice of creating special innovation budgets at the head-office level that people with good ideas can access year-round. Others have created dedicated innovation positions for people who work as in-house business angels, acting as sponsors and catalysts for new ideas.

However, if you are *not* working in such a company, your people may quickly run into a frequent political challenge, that of securing extra, nonbudgeted funds for an unforeseen but promising idea. We offer two possible strategies to address this:

- Tap into existing corporate initiatives. In large companies, it is often possible to use existing head-office initiatives to provide air cover for a local idea. For instance, when Cohen created pfizerWorks, Pfizer's then CEO Henry McKinnell had launched a companywide initiative called "Adapting To Scale." The ATS initiative wasn't directly aimed at the kind of idea Cohen had, but he nonetheless managed to position his idea under the ATS umbrella, allowing him to spend part of his time and budget on it. Are there any ongoing initiatives in your business that can provide air cover for innovation initiatives? Or are there any local projects that you can siphon some resources from?

- Ask people to seek external funding. In 2009, Gregers Wedell-Wedellsborg, Thomas's brother, worked for the large broadcaster TV2, when some of his employees had the idea of developing content for mobile phones. At the time, however, there was no viable business model for mobile content, and even though the emerging mobile space was a recognized priority for the company, securing the necessary funding internally would be difficult. Instead, Gregers encouraged his team to go *outside* the company to find funding for their mobile initiatives. As it turned out, the Danish mobile operators (telcos) were very interested in collaborating, as the high-volume video content promised to increase their earnings on data traffic and boost smartphone sales. The telcos agreed to fund content development, and that initial experiment launched TV2's venture into the mobile content market. With basically no internal funding, TV2 became a first mover in mobile media and a market leader. The collaboration also closed the gap until the mobile ad market matured and became a sustainable business model. In a similar vein, can you get your people to identify potential external collaborators?

5. Help People Manage Their Personal Brand

As we were writing this book, we asked a friend, Anders Ørjan, how creative people fared in his company, a major law firm. Ørjan's answer was succinct: "In my company, being called creative is the kiss of death for your career."

While law firms may be at the extreme end of the scale, Ørjan's comment reveals something important. Branding isn't just for products or firms. People also have *personal* brands, and much as our society may have a communal love affair with "the crazy ones," as Apple's famous ad called them—the rebels, the mavericks, the iconoclasts—the reality is that in many companies, being stereotyped as a creative person can be a mixed blessing. If you think of a classic "creative type," some positive terms will crop up: imaginative, thinks differently, willing to challenge norms. But, importantly, the stereotype is also imbued with some more dubious qualities, such as flaky, unstable, never arrives on time, and "often rocks the boat." As a 2010 study by Jennifer S. Mueller, Jack Goncalo, and Dishan Kamdar established, those clashing stereotypes can have negative consequences, because creative types are generally believed to have low leadership potential. (This is, of course, only a potential problem for those people who aspire to leadership positions.)

We raise this issue to highlight the need for *positioning*, both personally and on behalf of a particular project. As for personal branding, you have to look carefully at your company's culture: is it a place where creativity is well regarded? Or is it a place where people might benefit from stealthstorming instead, forgoing the Hawaiian shirt and the innovation buzzwords in favor of a steadier, more professional and businesslike reputation? (See also the box, "Stealthstorming and Creativity Training.")

Stealthstorming and Creativity Training

Does creativity training work? In 2004, Ginamarie Scott, Lyle Leritz, and Michael Mumford sought to answer that question by conducting a so-called meta-study of creativity training, a reliable type of study in which they reviewed and compiled seventy existing papers on the topic. The main finding of was that creativity training *does* work, which is good news, considering the untold number of employees who have attended such courses. The effect, the researchers found, is strongest for knowledge about creativity, and less strong (if still positive) for behavior.

However, the researchers also looked into the different *kinds* of training, and their analysis turned up something interesting. Specifically, they found that when training businesspeople, *artistic training methods were much less effective* than methods using business problems. In other words, what their study suggests is this: if you send people to a creativity training course, make sure it trains them in real-life problems, similar to those they face at work. Artsy, flamboyant methods that involve finger painting, improvised theater performances, and similar activities may deliver a great *experience* for the team—and can be worth including for that reason—but they are not likely to make them more creative. For that, you need to embrace the idea embodied in the notion of stealthstorming, namely, that to make innovation part of everyday life, it must be reinvented in an *un*exceptional form compatible with normal organizations. When pursuing innovation, go for realism, not escapism.

Conclusion: Suggested Action Items

This chapter has been about the fifth keystone behavior, *stealth-storming*. To increase the likelihood that people will succeed in clearing the organizational coral reefs, you can:

- Assist people in identifying and contacting potential sponsors in their networks, early in the process.

- Help your people craft a strong personal narrative about their ideas, sharing the essential benefits in a simple story.

- Consider if people can engineer personal experiences that demonstrate the value of the innovation, to increase the chance of converting key stakeholders.

- Consider the stealth trade-off between speed and safety: when is the right time to put a project on the corporate radar? Once on the radar, make sure people focus on demonstrating value as soon as possible.

- Have people search for internal and external sources of funds, including ongoing projects that might have spare resources. Push them to be creative on the issue of funding.

- Carefully assess the organizational climate, and have people consider their personal branding in that light. Will a creative reputation be an asset to people, or should they adopt a more low-key approach?

CHAPTER 7

PERSIST

HOW TO INCREASE PEOPLE'S PERSONAL MOTIVATION TO INNOVATE

CREATIVITY IS A CHOICE

Leaders must help their people persist in the pursuit
of innovation

In one of the modern world's first enquiries into great inno-vators, the nineteenth-century statesman and writer Robert Bulwer-Lytton became interested in the difference between talent and success. What intrigued Bulwer-Lytton was the fact that the world seemed to have an abundant supply of talented people. Yet, despite their obvious gifts, few ever seemed to accomplish anything truly significant. What kept these gifted people from turning their talent into success? What separated them from the true luminaries—people who had *delivered* on their talent?

Bulwer-Lytton's answer was simple: what set the success-ful people apart from others was not a superior intellect or a natural ability, but something much more mundane: their *persistence*. The common denominator of history's great men and women was simply that they *did not give up*. In the face of all the hardship that the world threw at them, these people were unyielding, keeping at it long after most ordinary mortals would have given up and started looking for the remote control.*

Two Ways to Foster Persistence

Persistence is of crucial relevance for managers. Scientific studies, both past and present, pay a lot of heed to *what* innovators do, and in this book, we have shared five keystone behaviors that leaders have to foster in their people. What Bulwer-Lytton's message adds to that is a final, critical insight: as important as *what* innovators do is the fact that they *keep* doing it. Making people engage in the five keystone behaviors once or twice won't bring you to innovation as usual. To achieve that, there is the sixth, overarching keystone behavior you have to promote: that of being *persistent*. For this reason, in this final chapter, we now turn to the topic of personal motivation and how to foster it in your people. Following the lead of motivation research, we

---

*The point is captured in Bulwer-Lytton's perhaps most famous quote, written under the pseudonym Owen Meredith: "Genius does what it must, and talent does what it can," from his poem "Last Words," published in the Victorian literary journal *The Cornhill Magazine*, November 1860. Bulwer-Lytton believed that geniuses were persistent because of a personal compulsion, but the point remains: persistence is essential to success.

zoom in on two specific drivers of people's actions that you can leverage to help them persist:

1. Love the journey: leverage intrinsic motivation

2. Check the destination: don't ignore extrinsic rewards

1. Love the Journey: Leverage Intrinsic Motivation

The notion of creating an architecture of innovation can be likened to *paving the way* for people, shaping the environment so the creative path becomes easier to travel. However, architecture can only take you so far, and there will always be obstacles you can't remove. Ultimately, people must *choose* to take—and stay on—the creative path, which brings us to the issue of *motivation*. In contrast to the concept of choice architecture, which is essentially about impersonal, external influences on behavior, motivation can be considered a personal, internal driver of what people do.

Researchers traditionally distinguish between *intrinsic* and *extrinsic* forms of motivation. Intrinsic motivation is when you enjoy an activity for its own sake; eating good food, going skiing, or socializing with friends are good examples, as are any professional activities you take pleasure in. Extrinsic motivation is when you don't particularly enjoy the activity itself, but do it to achieve something else, such as money or a promotion. Referring back to Frost's image of the two roads in the wood, intrinsic motivation is about the *journey*—how enjoyable is it to travel along the creative path?—whereas extrinsic motivation is about the *destination*: where will the creative path take me?

Of those two factors, we first consider how you can leverage people's intrinsic motivation.

Get People to Activate Their Personal Expertise

Previously, we explained the importance of helping people focus on opportunity spaces that matter to the business. This impersonal business-driven perspective, however, is not the only determinant of where you should have people look for ideas. Equally important, both for motivation and quality, is the matter of personal interests. If you think about one of your employees, *what does that person already love doing?* If someone is deeply passionate about, say, mobile technology, then it's probably a good idea to have him or her try to innovate in that space. In management, we often talk about how leaders motivate their people, using various forms of carrots and sticks. However, this is mostly appropriate for extrinsic motivation. With intrinsic motivation, leaders don't really motivate their people; it is more accurate to say that *people motivate themselves*. Leaders must try to create the conditions so this self-motivation can take place, directing it toward a goal that matters to the business.*

In many companies, people aren't asked to innovate in their own area of expertise, especially if that expertise is internal to the company. At some innovation events, we have seen managers force their people to brainstorm on new products or services *for their customers only*, while deliberately avoiding any discussion of possibilities for internal innovation. Focusing

---

*If you'll permit us to build on the classic analogy without imputing equine characteristics to anyone: if you have a donkey that loves eating grass, you need neither carrots nor sticks. All you need to do is aim the donkey at an untended lawn and then charge the homeowner for the lawn mowing.

everybody's innovation efforts on the customer can be fruitful *if* people happen to have a solid grasp of what their customers' lives are like. But if you are dealing with a group of forty-something finance people working deep in the bowels of the organization, their chances of coming up with a *useful* customer innovation are severely limited. If some people simply aren't in touch with the company's customers, it is often considerably more fruitful to have them innovate in areas they already know.

Have People Connect to What They Know and Love

Having people search for ideas in areas they know carries two additional benefits besides increased motivation. First, it is a way to get more *original* ideas. As creativity researcher Mark Runco has found, if you instruct people to look for ideas *that only they could come up with*, they will produce more unusual, off-kilter ideas because they activate their own, private knowledge. Second, in her pioneering diary-based studies of creativity in organizations, Teresa Amabile found that people are more likely to have useful ideas if they have what is called *domain expertise*, that is, an in-depth understanding of the area they are trying to innovate within.*

---

*While originality and usefulness seem similar, these two advantages are not the same thing. In particular, *originality* is a dual-edged sword: an original idea may not have been discovered by others, but originality also means untried, untested, and risky. In the television business, for instance, commissioning editors may say they look for "original" ideas for new TV shows, but often, what they really want are ideas within a safe, proven genre that are *just* different enough from the existing offerings to avoid legal copyright skirmishes. This dark side of real originality is the raison d'être of the market for television formats like *Who Wants to Be a Millionaire* and similar. (For more on this, see Thomas Wedell-Wedellsborg, *The Market for Television Formats,* http://www.IAsUsual.com.)

When we work with managers, we like to translate these insights into the following rules of thumb (see figure 7-1):

1. Have people look for ideas in areas they *know and love.*

2. Within that, have people look for ideas with *potential value* to the business.

The logic of this is straightforward. When people are passionate about a specific domain, constantly trying to improve their own mastery of it, they are much more likely to *persist* with their ideas, driving to overcome the inevitable setbacks. When people know the domain intimately, their ideas are also much more likely to be both valuable and feasible. Finally, by asking them to somehow connect those ideas to the objectives of the business, you reduce the risk that they pick a pet project to work on that does not align with the company's strategy.

FIGURE 7-1

Domains for useful ideas

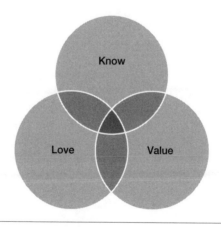

(Persistence becomes a bad trait if people chase ideas that have no hope of creating value for the business.)*

Give People Autonomy, Purpose, and Teammates

Daniel Pink, in his book *Drive,* explains that besides the desire to master an area of expertise, people are also motivated by having a clear purpose and by having autonomy, that is, the power to decide their own actions.

Providing purpose to people can be as simple as emphasizing that their idea serves the larger aims of the organization, whether saving lives, improving the world, or something similar. However, that larger purpose need not be of an epic nature. In a company we worked for, for instance, the managers wanted to connect people across the organizational silos, with the aim of improving internal coordination. As they explained the reasons for the new initiative to their employees, the managers didn't just highlight the expected benefits to the business. They also emphasized another important aspect of the initiative: it would allow people to get to know their colleagues better, strengthening the collegial spirit in the office. Having a sense of purpose does not have to be about saving the world; it can also be about more mundane, but still worthy aims.

As for autonomy, the more freedom you can give people to run with their innovation ideas, the more motivated they are likely to be. Importantly, though, research has shown that this autonomy does not have to be about the objectives; people don't

---

*This last requirement, demonstrating potential value, should be loosened if you are looking for longer-term ideas or potential game changers, as the value of those ideas will rarely be evident to start with. As mentioned, however, this is also a much riskier strategy and is rarely appropriate for regular business units.

mind chasing after externally defined ends as long as those ends generally make sense. What matters is that they can determine the *means* themselves and aren't micromanaged in how they should approach the task of realizing the idea.

Finally, if you were to head alone into a dark wood, chances are you'd be tempted to turn back quickly, whereas the presence of some trusted travel companions would significantly lighten the mood. One of the most powerful levers for helping people persist in pursuing an idea is to form a small, close-knit team around it. So, if your people do not seek out a few allies themselves, make sure to connect them with one or two other people to work on the idea, leveraging the power of social motivation.

NutroFoods Belgium Revisited

We saw the power of intrinsic motivation firsthand as we worked with Marc Granger at NutroFoods Belgium, the case we discussed in chapter 1. As Granger worked to drive cultural change in the subsidiary, he chose to focus strongly on fostering intrinsic motivation in his people, with great success. How he did that merits some attention, because as a leader, if you want to leverage internal motivation, you have to strike the right balance between freedom and control.

First, while Granger let people pick and drive their own innovation projects, he didn't give total freedom. From the start, he was clear on one thing: the projects they chose had to support the overall aim, namely of making NutroFoods a better and more innovative workplace. The management team had carefully chosen this strategic aim; the business was suffering due to the high employee turnover, so it would be beneficial to lower it while also making people take more initiatives and be open to doing things differently. As he set the process in motion, Granger explained to his people that he reserved the right to challenge and stop projects if they could not explain how it would help them achieve the objective.

Within that overall constraint, however, Granger did his best to give people the maximum possible opportunity to follow their own passions and interests. He didn't require them to work on something that was customer-facing; quite the contrary, if people wanted to work on an internal issue, as many of them did, they were free to do so. Furthermore, he did *not* require everybody to work on a project. His philosophy was simple: "This can't be a management-driven thing. I told my people, you have to pick a project that you truly believe in and think is worth doing. If you don't want to participate, that's okay. If you don't feel strongly enough about an idea to invest your time in it, then it's probably not worth doing. This is about letting your passion drive you—not your boss. It is an opportunity to build a better workplace for yourself and your colleagues—but you have to seize that opportunity."

Walking the Talk

At first, people were hesitant to believe that Granger would really give them freedom to pick their own projects. As we spoke to the employees, several admitted to initially thinking that it was all just window dressing, and expected managers to drive and define the projects as they had done in the past. Granger described one instance: "In one of the groups, the project leaders came up after some time and asked us 'what had been decided.' They were clearly expecting us to tell them which projects we thought they should pursue. We told them, 'Nothing. It is up to you to decide what initiatives you want to focus on, and to ask for the budget you would need.' That drove the point home, I think."

As Granger and his team kept reinforcing the message through their actions, people gradually started believing it. A crucial moment came when the proposal to do a work-life balance program came up. Many people had wanted to focus on work-life balance—often a sensitive topic with managers—and one of the teams had suggested hiring an external coach to train people in it. Granger initially resisted the idea; when the team brought him the proposal, Granger challenged them about whether it made sense. But it soon became clear that his people were truly passionate about the project and were willing to fight in order to make it happen. That was exactly the kind of passion that Granger had been hoping to foster. So he eventually authorized the budget. As one of the employees told us: "The kickoff had been a really good day, but to be honest, it hadn't convinced me that the management was truly serious about changing things. But I started believing it when the project groups were actually given real resources to do things with. In my group, the management authorized our proposal and our budget, and allowed us to spend six times three working hours on the work-life balance pilot program. *That* made me believe that they were serious about wanting to change things."

Interestingly, the work-life balance project ended up being a major driver of NutroFoods Belgium's success. As the experiment proceeded, it became clear that Granger's people could manage the new freedom responsibly and, in fact, used it to become even more productive. One employee told us, "I have actually worked *more* since we shifted to the new model. But I work when it suits me, I can pick up the kids from school outside of rush hour, and I enjoy it more." Eventually, as the initiative developed, it became so successful at delivering better results and new ideas that several other countries in Europe decided to implement it.

Most significantly, Grangers's ability to leverage the intrinsic motivation of his people made the initiative *endure*. As the process was well underway, a job opening unexpectedly materialized higher up in the organization, and Granger was promoted ahead of schedule, forcing him to leave NutroFoods Belgium after only two years. At this point, most other innovation projects would likely have foundered, not least those driven by top management. But because Granger had managed to create a true sense of ownership in his people, they persisted in the pursuit of the new culture despite his absence. Four years and three country managers later, the innovation (and the results) at NutroFoods Belgium is still going strong. (See also the box, "Intrinsic Motivation and Choke Points.")

2. Check the Destination: Don't Ignore Extrinsic Rewards

Intrinsic motivation is only part of the picture; the flip side is the role of extrinsic motivation, that is, the rewards that may accrue to innovators, such as bonuses, promotions, and other objects of worldly desire. In addition to the intrinsic joy people may derive from the journey along the creative path, what will happen to them when they reach the destination? Or, for that matter, what will happen if they tread the path but fail to reach the destination, in the many cases when otherwise promising ideas simply don't work out?

Intrinsic Motivation and Choke Points

The great advantage of intrinsic motivation is that it can make people deal with even severe obstacles, taking persistence to a level that neither architecture nor rewards can ultimately match. However, the energy needed to cross barriers is better spent moving forward, and there may be certain choke points on the creative path that you should seek to alleviate or remove. As you look at that path, ask yourself: Are there any weak or broken links in the innovation value chain? Is it, for instance, easy to connect with colleagues, but very hard to gain access to funding? Is it overly difficult to seek the necessary formal approvals for new ideas? Is it all but impossible to run small experiments? For each of the main elements of the process, you need to consider whether there are any bottlenecks in the behavioral architecture. Generally speaking, it is *not* possible to create perfect conditions for innovation, considering that it is not your first priority. But it *is* possible to make the creative path a little smoother on critical junctures. By addressing the worst passages and bridging a gap here and there, innovation architects can make tremendous leaps of progress.

Interestingly, in creativity and innovation, the role of extrinsic motivation is hotly contested. Many researchers are proponents of the *art for art's sake* theory of motivation, that is, the belief that with creativity, people are not motivated by extrinsic rewards like money or promotions, but more by the intrinsic joys of engaging in the creative act. This belief is almost a religion unto itself in the world of fine art, a domain in which being "in it for the money" is considered outright mercenary, a hallmark of lesser artists. In the business domain, too, it has strong backing, with many scientific studies confirming that intrinsic motivation is important, to a point where some have concluded that extrinsic rewards are outright dangerous. Consider this piece of advice from a recent research paper on creativity: "Do not let yourself be captivated by extrinsic motivation (e.g., money) as reward for creative productions— money corrupts! In general, the motivation for creative acts should come from within the person (intrinsic motivation)."

With statements like these, coming in many cases from esteemed and well-researched sources, many managers may think that, for their people, creative work should be its own reward. But while most of the research is valid, there is a catch or two in it. As we argue here, there are good reasons to revisit reward systems for innovators and see if you should improve them.

Innovation Is Hard Work

There is a big difference between creativity and innovation: because of the need for implementation, innovation tends to involve more hard work. When we think of innovation, we tend to assume people are engaged in enjoyable creative behavior: sitting and getting ideas, tinkering with a new product, dreaming up grand visions, brainstorming. But that is not the case. For instance, as we looked at the actions Jordan Cohen took to build pfizerWorks, it became clear that few of those activities were primarily *creative* actions. The pfizerWorks service itself was certainly a creative labor, considered as a whole, but when you look at the component parts, it is clear that many of them are not creative, nor are they particularly enjoyable on their own: Building and managing a team. Seeking political support. Creating and managing a budget. Preparing presentations. Soliciting and incorporating feedback. Conducting due diligence. The list effectively reads like an exercise in Project Management 101. For all these actions, people may be creative about *how* they do it, just as they can be creative when it comes to performing their regular jobs. But nothing in the nature of the tasks themselves is particularly creative in the sense that we tend to think about enjoyable, creative work. This suggests that while innovators may have little regard for extrinsic rewards early on in the process, those factors are likely to become more salient as time passes and the labor becomes characterized more by implementation and maintenance-oriented work.

This has been our personal experience as well. As Wedell-Wedellsborg built his second start-up, a professional network for top-tier business schools called 13 MBAs, intrinsic motivation played a huge role in the beginning. However, as time went on, and as more and more humdrum work crept in, intrinsic motivation faded somewhat, yielding to more menial extrinsic motivations like the need to earn money. Intrinsic motivation is great for getting things started. Extrinsic motivation may matter a lot more for getting things finished.

Varying Thresholds for Innovative Behavior

While many argue in favor of the art-for-art's-sake theory, there are also prominent dissenting voices among the researchers. One such dissenter is Robert Sternberg, a leading creativity scholar and a former dean at Tufts University. Together with his colleague Todd Lubart, Sternberg coined the so-called "investment theory" of creativity, a perspective emphasizing that promoting innovation is not just a question of increasing people's creative potential. It can equally be seen as a question of promoting their willingness to *use* that potential. In one of his papers, Sternberg says: "Our fundamental premise is that creativity is in large part a decision that anyone can make but that few people actually do make because they find the costs to be too high." In another paper, he puts it like this: "People may fail to be radically creative not because they lack the knowledge but rather because they lack the desire to experience the kind of rejection that radical creativity often brings with it."

What Sternberg points out is that people have different thresholds for taking creative action. On one hand, there are people like Virgin's Richard Branson who will innovate no matter what happens. Should Branson ever have the misfortune of being wrongfully incarcerated for a few days, you can be sure that his empire will soon include a chain of Virgin correctional facilities. On the other hand, most people are more hesitant to innovate than that. If your workplace is anything like the organizations we have worked with, then for every unstoppable, die-hard creative type like Branson, you've probably got fifty to a hundred employees who *can* be innovative if the conditions are right. But what is key about these people is that they won't do it if the personal cost of persistence is too high: they may be creative, but they are not fools. So, given that regular managers can't just replace their people with creative superstars—we do need to get some real work done in between all the innovation—it can often make more sense, as Sternberg counsels, to work on "increasing the rewards and decreasing the costs" of taking individual creative action.

Rewards Are Hygiene Factors

Even if Sternberg and the other proponents of extrinsic rewards should turn out to be wrong, there is still an aspect of motivation that most people agree on, namely, the status of rewards as *hygiene factors*, a concept that was formulated by the early management scholar, Frederick Herzberg. What the notion of hygiene factors (i.e., job security, salary, benefits, and so on) conveys is that some elements, while not actively motivating in themselves, can still create *dis*satisfaction if they are below a certain threshold or are considered grossly unfair in comparison to peers.

Consider the issue of career paths for innovators. As a team of researchers from Rensselaer Polytechnic Institute found, most companies don't provide good career opportunities for in-house innovators. One of the research subjects, a member of an innovation hub in a large consumer products company, explained: "I could help launch $4, $5, $6 billion businesses over the next five years, and I won't get promoted into leadership for this company." Given such a state of affairs, one can't really blame people if they forget about innovation and seek safer ways to get promoted, such as sticking to business as usual.

In your company, how will innovators fare in terms of money, careers, and prestige, compared to people who stick with business as usual? What the hygiene-factor perspective suggests is that innovators don't necessarily need to do better than people who do business as usual, but if they do considerably worse, then many people won't innovate. In your business, are people effectively punished for innovating?

Define Failure Carefully

Closely related is the matter of defining acceptable failure (or acceptable loss). One of the many notions from Brainstorm Island is that we should "celebrate failure," but, when managers heed this advice unthinkingly, they can get in a lot of trouble. For instance, Robert, a manager we worked with, said in a speech to his people that their company and their management team "would become better at celebrating failures." People liked hearing this, of course, but, two months later, Robert had to fire some of his salespeople for ethical misconduct. This created a serious backlash among the employees, many of whom found Robert hypocritical.

Failure is a companion of innovation, but it is not in and of itself a good thing, and "celebrating" it, unless done properly, can quickly seem insincere or out of tune with the corporate culture. For this reason, managers must define what *kind* of failure is (and is not) accepted, specifying how people should distinguish between the two. Robert wasn't wrong in firing the salespeople, nor was he wrong in encouraging people to experiment with new ideas. His mistake was that he didn't explain what he meant by "failure" in the first place. Just as innovation architects have to define success when creating the innovation strategy, they need to clarify what failure is acceptable and what is not. (See the box, "Should Innovation Be Risky for Employees?")

Should Innovation Be Risky for Employees?

Some innovation experts suggest that companies should make pursuing innovation risk-free, effectively letting the company shoulder all risks and rewarding innovators regardless of whether or not they fail.

We believe the matter is more nuanced. Innovation *is* inherently riskier than business as usual, and there is nothing good about risk. In inventing the light bulb, Thomas Edison may have had the resources to fail ten thousand times, but that's probably not the case for you or your people. Given the downside of dropping the ball on your regular business obligations, giving people carte blanche to innovate may create an unfortunate incentive to embrace too much risk. For this reason, as long as the punishment for failing isn't too debilitating, there is nothing wrong with letting your people share *some* of the risk of innovating. One way to position the choice to innovate is to have your people think about it as a higher-risk, higher-reward career path, compared to business as usual. If the personal risks and rewards of innovation are properly balanced, the choice to innovate will be attractive to some, but not all, of your employees, which is exactly what you should be aiming for, at least for innovation projects that go beyond the purely incremental.

In summary, when it comes to rewards, consider your group of employees and then focus on the large majority in the middle. This group has the real potential for fostering more innovation, because for them, creativity is neither an impossibility nor a compulsion. For them, creativity is a choice. So what makes people make that choice? On the one hand, being sensible people, they want a reasonable assurance that they will not get lost in the woods. If they, standing at the crossroads, can see that the creative path is littered with corpses of innovators past, they are going to drop their ideas and go straight back to business as usual. If, on the other hand, there are clear signs that successful innovators are rewarded, that failed innovators aren't treated *too* badly, and that current, ongoing innovators are not made to go through hell, then they just might take the creative path more often, embracing innovation as usual.

Conclusion: Suggested Action Items

In this chapter, we've discussed the overarching keystone behavior, helping people *persist*. To make it more likely that your employees will keep searching for innovation, as a regular part of their work lives, here are some pointers:

- Find ways of tapping into the intrinsic motivation people already possess. Can you pair up people with opportunity spaces that align with what they know and love? Given this, can you direct them so they focus on strategic priorities?

- Examine the extrinsic rewards for innovators (including those who fail), and compare them to how noninnovators fare. Is there a reasonable relationship between them?

- Can you do limited experiments with the various incentives to innovate in order to learn what works in your situation and for your people?

THE MONDAY MORNING PROBLEM

WHAT YOU DO IN THE NEXT TWENTY MINUTES IS THE DIFFERENCE BETWEEN FAILURE AND SUCCESS

Just like ideas, books need to be more than thought provoking. To have impact, they need to be *action* provoking as well. If they fail in this, no matter how excellent otherwise, all they create is a warm and fuzzy feeling that will swiftly fade away to nothingness. For this reason we want to end the book by telling you about the single biggest danger to innovation. We call it the *Monday morning problem*, and it relates to what you do right after putting down this book. Specifically, what you do in the next twenty minutes of your life may well be crucial to your success as an innovation architect.

The Monday morning problem is a phenomenon we personally came to understand as we first started running executive education courses. On the last day of the courses, typically a Friday, the participants would be all fired up about innovation, full of ideas and plans for how to make it happen in their companies. (You may have felt this way if you've ever taken part in a good course or workshop.) But later, when we followed up on what the participants had been doing after the course, we found that many of them never realized *any* of their plans. What had thwarted their ambitions was not a lack of insights or ideas, or any of the other matters we have described in the book. It was simpler still, and more deadly: they had never gotten started. Like New Year's resolutions, their budding desire to innovate had wilted once exposed to the harsh glare of everyday life. Monday morning had gotten them.

The essence of the Monday morning problem is that, in a sense, you are not really a single, consistent person. Rather, scholars of behavioral research are concluding that, in some ways, we are all suffering from a mild type of multiple personality disorder: depending on the time and the situation, we carry around several different personalities, each with different aims and desires. People who try to lose weight know the feeling; one part of you wants to get healthy, shape up, and look decent in a bathing suit. The other part of you just wants a cookie. Too often, when we are standing in front of the pastry display and the moment of truth arrives, the cookie-loving self is in the driver's seat, whereas the health freak is tied up in the trunk.

On our executive education programs, we solved the Monday morning problem only when we started addressing it specifically, adding things like mentor programs and one-hundred-day follow-up systems to the program, things that are a bit hard to include in a book. For this reason, we have a simple, practical question for you: if you have decided to pursue innovation, what should be your next step? Looking at the next five to ten business days, how will you make sure that it happens?

If your answer is "willpower," you may be in trouble. It is dangerous to think that your own determination and drive will be enough to escape the inertia of business as usual. We know not just from experience, but also from research that self-discipline does not have a strong track record. Chances are that once you put down this book and hit Monday morning, you too will be caught up in the strong and unforgiving currents of your everyday job. The starting point for becoming an innovation architect is therefore to take a look at your own situation: What is stopping *you*, personally, from focusing on innovation? And what can you do about it? How can you stop yourself from becoming yet another victim of the Monday morning problem?

We propose a single, effective remedy: get *one* other person involved. Time and again, when we look at the successful innovation architects from our studies, they started their journey toward innovation as usual with a single step: getting someone else involved. Later, all of these managers would build more and stronger innovation routines into their lives, but they all started with the magical factor: one other person.

So, our final suggestions are:

1. Make a simple plan now. Spend the next five to ten minutes planning the first step. Make a specific plan, with date and time, about what you will do next.

2. Find a partner. Identify someone in your workplace who can be your partner in crime. The person can be anyone: a colleague, a subordinate, or a superior you have a good relationship with. The key thing is that

this person is part of your daily environment, so you have opportunities to have quick, informal meetings and can help each other maintain momentum.

3. Set up the first meeting before you put down this book. Within twenty minutes from now, you should have contacted that person. Call him or her, set up a meeting or a lunch, have coffee together. And, of course, consider buying the person a copy of this book, so you can be on the same page conceptually. (Heck, buy it for your entire company.)

Most of all, keep it simple. Don't try to involve three or four people. Start with one or, at most, two. Including more than a few people creates a need for formally scheduling meetings, which will kill your momentum.

With this final piece of advice, you are now well armed to take on the role of innovation architect, leading the journey toward a better, brighter, and more creative future. We hope that you will soon revel in the full potential of your people, seeing them go forth into corporate tomorrows, bringing great ideas to life.

Paddy Miller
Thomas Wedell-Wedellsborg
New York City, March 2013

APPENDIX A

FURTHER READING

In this appendix, we recommend some books for readers who want or need to delve further into the innovation literature. We have deliberately chosen to limit the number of recommendations on each topic; it is our experience that if you recommend one book, people just might read it, but if you recommend ten books, chances are they won't read any of them. The list is also available on our website (www.IAsUsual.com) with direct links to the various books and articles.

Focus

The notion of directing the search for innovation covers many aspects, from setting clear goals to developing a full-fledged innovation strategy. Here are some good resources for delving further into this aspect of the search for innovation.

- **Strategy in general.** In his article, "Can You Say What Your Strategy Is?" (*Harvard Business Review*, April 2008), David J. Collis, a coauthor with the late Michael G. Rukstad, provides a simple, powerful framework for what a strategy really is and how managers can communicate it. While they do not discuss innovation as such, the article is important reading if you (or your colleagues) don't have a clear, shared, and operational understanding of strategy.

- Innovation strategy. One author who has tackled innovation strategy in various books and articles is Scott Anthony, in particular, in the book *The Innovator's Guide to Growth*, coauthored with Mark Johnson, Joseph Sinfield, and Elizabeth Altman (2008, Harvard Business Press). The authors focus mostly on developing new services and products for customers (and noncustomers), and talk less about internal innovation, but the book is well worth reading.

- Business models. A good resource for mapping your business model is provided by Alex Osterwelder and Yves Pigneur in *Business Model Generation* (2010, Wiley), in which Osterwelder, Pigneur, and their many coauthors have developed the so-called business model canvas.

- Journeys. An alternative is simply to map out the different journeys that occur in your organization: products as they flow through the organization, customers as they come into contact with your product, or your people as they work together across the organization. Mapping each journey can help you identify new areas to look for innovation.

Connect

The keystone behavior of *connecting* builds on many different frameworks, covering ideation, ethnographic methods, open innovation, and more.

- Technology brokering and recombinant innovation. Andrew Hargadon's *How Breakthroughs Happen* (2003, Harvard Business School Press) is an in-depth guide to the study of where new ideas come from and how businesses can get better at finding them.

- Studying consumers and finding pain points. We recommend two classics and one more recent book for understanding more about consumer research:

  - *Hidden in Plain Sight* by Erich Joachimsthaler (2007, Harvard Business School Press) provides a strong, in-depth guide to the various ways of studying consumers and customers. It is an excellent read for people who are going to work with ethnography professionally.

  - *Why We Buy: The Science of Shopping* by Paco Underhill (1999, Simon & Schuster), provides a riveting case study into people's shopping behaviors, detailing the power (and commercial application) of ethnography. Your view of narrow shopping aisles will never be the same again.

  - *The Design of Everyday Things* by Donald A. Norman (2002, Basic Books) is another classic that should be required reading for everybody. It is an excellent introduction to basic pain points; for instance, in how many bad ways can you design a *door*?

- Getting ideas from the outside

  - Vijay Govindarajan and Chris Trimble's book *Reverse Innovation* (2012, Harvard Business Review Press) shares thought-provoking examples of how companies tap into developing markets to find radical new ideas.

  - For a study of how one (big) company implemented open innovation, read A. G. Lafley and Ram Charan's *The Game Changer* (2008, Crown Business). Clay Shirky's books on collaboration are also worthwhile, e.g., *Here Comes Everybody* (2008, Penguin Press).

  - Richard Florida's work on cities as engines of creativity provides a different take on collaborative innovation; start with his *Rise of the Creative Class* (the revised second edition, published in 2012 by Basic Books), or check out his blog on the website of The Atlantic (http://www.theatlanticcities.com/).

- Intersections. Frans Johansson's book *The Medici Effect* (2004, Harvard Business School Press) provides hands-on advice on how to access completely new fields of knowledge; it is written in a highly entertaining, Gladwell-esque style. His new book *The Click Moment* is also worth reading (2012, Portfolio Hardcover).

- Office layout. For those interested in the physical architecture of the workplace, Thomas J. Allen and Gunter Henn's book, *The Organization and Architecture of*

Innovation, is an illustrated tour of how various companies have changed their office layouts in order to promote interaction and cross-fertilization among people (2006, Butterworth-Heinemann).

Tweak

- **Mapping assumptions.** In *Discovery-Driven Growth* (2009, Harvard Business Press), Rita McGrath and Ian MacMillan provide a practical, business-minded framework for working with fuzzy ideas and clarifying hidden assumptions. Great for businesspeople who want to work more systematically with idea development.

- **Customer development and pivoting.** Steve Blank and his concepts of customer development, pivoting and more are both gospel and shibboleth for the Silicon Valley start-up crowd. See his blog at www.steveblank.com to get a feel for his ideas, and if you like them, consider getting his *Four Steps to the Epiphany* (2005, Cafepress.com). Eric Ries's *The Lean Startup* (2011, Crown Business) is also worth reading.

- **Prototyping and design thinking.** The various books from IDEO are great starting points, not least the classics *The Art of Innovation* (2001, Crown Business) and *The Ten Faces of Innovation* (2005, Currency/Doubleday), both written by Tom Kelley and Jonathan Littman. Tim Brown's more recent *Change by Design* (2009, HarperBusiness) is also a good introduction to the discipline.

- Reframing the problem. Hands-on tools for reframing are not abundantly available in the business literature, but some good starting points are:

  - The HBR article, "Breakthrough Thinking from Inside the Box," by Kevin P. Coyne, Patricia Gorman Clifford, and Renée Dye provides practical examples and guidance on how to reframe the search for ideas (December 2007), as does another HBR article, "Are You Solving the Right Problem?" by Dwayne Spradlin (September 2012).

  - Clayton Christensen and Michael Raynor's book, *The Innovator's Solution* (2003, Harvard Business School Press), details the "jobs to be done" framework, which is a good tool for analyzing and rethinking consumer needs in detail.

- Tweaking. "The Tweaker," Malcolm Gladwell's *New Yorker* article from November 2011 on Steve Jobs, provides food for thought and some examples of tweaking in action. Walter Isaacson's eponymous biography of Steve Jobs is also excellent and inspiring (2011, Simon & Schuster).

Select

- An overview of idea selection. For newcomers to the discipline of idea selection, we recommend starting with Joe Tidd and John Bessant's *Managing Innovation* (2009, Wiley), especially chapters 7 to 9, which give an excellent overview of the various tools, techniques, and approaches currently in use.

- Innovation value chain. Morten T. Hansen and Julian Birkinshaw's HBR article, "The Innovation Value Chain," from June 2007 shares some important insights on idea filtering and a useful diagnostic framework that can help assess your company's innovation ecosystem.

- Metrics and reward systems. *Making Innovation Work*, by Tony Davila, Marc Epstein, and Robert Shelton (2005, Pearson Prentice Hall) is a systematic and hands-on guide to the links among strategy, processes, metrics, and incentives surrounding corporate innovation.

- More on innovation metrics. Chapter 10 of *The Innovators Guide to Growth* by Scott D. Anthony, Mark W. Johnson, Joseph V. Sinfield, and Elizabeth J. Altman provides a clear-eyed discussion of innovation metrics and some of the associated pitfalls (2008, Harvard Business Press).

- Innovation tournaments. Christian Terwiesch and Karl Ulrich's book *Innovation Tournaments* (2009, Harvard Business Press) provides detail on a specific type of idea filtering, namely creating idea competitions akin to the talent shows on TV. The book contains several important lessons on filtering ideas.

- Stage-gate processes. Robert G. Cooper's body of work on new product development is a deep wellspring of information for people who need to set up stage-gate processes and similar, complex filtering systems. Start at the website of Cooper and his colleague Scott Edgett: www.prod-dev.com.

- Decision biases. Of the numerous books on human decision biases, Daniel Kahneman's *Thinking, Fast and Slow* (2011, Farrar, Straus and Giroux) is one of the best and most thought-provoking.

- Crowdsourcing. While not a business book, *The Wisdom of Crowds* by James Surowiecki (2004, Doubleday) is a good introduction to the fundamentals of using crowds to filter ideas.

Stealthstorm

- Innovating in big organizations. Vijay Govindarajan and Chris Trimble's *The Other Side of Innovation* (2010, Harvard Business Review Press) provides clear-eyed, practical advice on the dangers and shortcuts in running innovation projects in large, political companies, with a particular focus on the oft-ignored implementation phase.

- Innovation in practice. Scott Anthony's *The Little Black Book of Innovation* (2011, Harvard Business Review Press) guides the reader through twenty-eight useful lessons on innovation, sharing several insights about navigating the political landscape. Very hands-on and accessible; great for busy practitioners.

- Storytelling. Klaus Fog and Christian Budtz's *Storytelling: Branding in Practice* (2010, Springer) provides some hands-on tools and techniques for crafting and sharing effective stories, particularly with the aim of marketing and branding.

- Power. Jeffrey Pfeffer's *Power: Why Some People Have It and Others Don't* (2010, HarperBusiness) is an excellent guide to understanding organizational realpolitik.

- Communication. *Made to Stick* by Chip Heath and Dan Heath (2007, Random House) also gives invaluable advice on shaping effective communication.

Persist

The chapter on persistence is strongly informed by research on behavior change.

- Motivation in general. Daniel Pink's book *Drive* (2009, Riverhead) gives an easily accessible introduction to motivation, with a particular focus on creative behavior and hands-on recommendations.

- Motivation at work. Teresa Amabile's work on motivation is one of the most rigorous studies of daily creativity in organizations. Her recent book with Steven Kramer, *The Progress Principle*, highlights how managers can increase motivation by enabling people's progress (2011, Harvard Business Review Press).

- Changing behavior. Chip Heath and Dan Heath's *Switch* (2010, Crown Business) is one of the best books on the topic of behavior change. *Influencer* by Kerry Patterson, Joseph Grenny, David Maxfield, Ron McMillan, and Al Switzler is a great supplementary read (2007, McGraw-Hill).

- Forming habits. *The Power of Habit* by Charles Duhigg (2012, Random House) gives a good in-depth treatment of what habits are and how you can work on forming new ones.

- Nudges and choice architecture. *Nudge* by Richard H. Thaler and Cass R. Sunstein (2008, Yale University Press) provides a fascinating, wide-ranging study of nudges, choice architecture, and human biases; they focus mostly on issues related to government and public service, not businesses.

- Behavior design. B. J. Fogg's work on behavior design is a practical framework for thinking about—and modifying— people's behavior; to learn more, visit his website at www. bjfogg.com.

- Reward systems in general. Steve Kerr has written a short, hands-on book about reward systems, simply called *Reward Systems: Does Yours Measure Up?* (2008, Harvard Business Press). It is a practical guide for managers who are designing or tweaking their incentive systems.

INNOVATION DEFINED

The literature offers many different definitions of innovation, some more complex than others. To be practical, we like to use the following, easy-to-remember definition:

Innovation = Creating results by doing new things

Here are some key elements of our definition:

Innovation is about *action*. Some experts define innovation as a new product or service that is created; others focus on thinking differently. We take a behavioral perspective on innovation, focusing on the fact that people—your employees, partners, customers, or all three—need to *change their behavior* in order for innovation to happen. Helping people think differently is one thing; the real challenge is to help them *act* differently.

Innovation involves doing something *new* or different, and this, in a sense, is where the trouble starts. "Business as usual," that is, the opposite of innovation, is basically when people create results by doing *old, well-known* things, which is really great as long as they get the job done. The difficulties start when people have to go beyond business as usual, because "new" doesn't just mean exciting or promising, but also untried, untested, and therefore risky. Also, innovation doesn't need to be new to the entire world (in which case, it's probably very risky). For our purposes in this book, what counts is that innovation is new *to the people involved*, and that there are no established processes available for doing it.*

Innovation is about creating results. At the individual level, people may pursue innovation purely for its own sake. But from a business perspective, innovation is and should be a means to an end; it has to create value or fulfill a useful purpose. As we cover in chapter 2, defining that purpose— and making sure it connects to the overarching strategic objectives of the business—is an important part of what innovation architects do. Noticeably, "results" can mean different things depending on what your business does, say, growth, cost reductions, lives saved, increased sustainability, or even the survival of the business. But at the end of the day, innovation should make a measurable difference. As innovation expert Scott Anthony, another proponent of short definitions, puts it: "No impact, no innovation."

Working with Definitions in Practice

Defining innovation is not only relevant in the context of this book. It is also a practical matter, because early in any innovation

---

*For instance, you generally don't need innovation skills to implement an enterprise software system in your business, because that is by and large a well-understood process with clear step-by-step guidelines. You may need therapy and/or a long vacation, though.

journey, someone will put a hand up and ask, "What exactly do you mean by innovation?"

You and your people need to have a shared understanding of what the word means. And because a definition is not a universal truth, but rather a tool that should be useful in the context of your specific situation, agreeing on the exact, detailed definition will require some discussion among the people who are going to make it happen. Therein lies the danger of "paralysis by analysis," not least if some of your employees happen to enjoy vigorously debating minor points (and really, who doesn't?). We have seen a few leaders get derailed in meetings because they opened up this particular Pandora's box too early and got lost in a haze of arguments about the finer terminological differences between "insights" and "ideas." The time and place for that discussion is rarely at the very beginning of the process.

For this reason, when you start out on the journey, we recommend sticking with the definition we provided. Think of this definition as a placeholder: one that allows people to start moving forward, and which will get the job done until it becomes necessary (and possible) to create a more detailed definition that will work for you. In the beginning, keep it simple, keep it moving.

FOUR GOOD REASONS TO INNOVATE

As a leader, your employees will sooner or later ask the question, "Why do we need to innovate?" Here are a few thoughts on what your answer should—and should not—be.

"In today's ever-slower, ever less competitive business environment . . ." Much as we would like to have started our book with this statement, we would have a hard time defending it. If you have spent time in organizations, chances are you have heard your fair share of burning-platform, innovate-or-die, remember-what-happened-to-the-dinosaurs sermons, all pointing out what most managers know by now, namely, that innovation is a key driver of growth, whereas *lack* of innovation will sooner or later have fatal consequences for a business.*

---

*On a side note, the popular invocation of dinosaurs as history's losers borders on the involuntarily amusing; it's not as if we mammals rose up and smartly outflanked the competition by way of routing a comet into the Earth. In fact, looking at the scoreboard of history, dinosaurs ruled the earth for millennia, dying off only because of a freak cosmic accident entirely beyond anyone's control. Humanity, in comparison, has ruled for a fraction of that time, and there are probably even odds that our eventual demise will be entirely self-orchestrated. Perhaps it is time to revise our lowly opinion of the dinosaurs?

These kinds of arguments are a staple of how managers try to motivate their people to innovate. We won't repeat any of them here, though, because, while they are true, they are largely *company* arguments, not people arguments. Ultimately, companies are abstractions; only people see, feel, live, and think, or are motivated to innovate. What that means is that making innovation happen isn't just about stepping into the suave loafers of the CEO and taking an eagle's-eye perspective on things. First, you must step into the shoes of your people to see the world with their eyes. Once you do that, it becomes clear that the real question is not, why is innovation important to the business, but why is innovation important to *them*? Why shouldn't your people just continue down the road of business as usual and leave innovation to somebody else? And for that matter, why shouldn't you?

We believe that there are at least four strong personal reasons to pursue innovation as usual; share these at your leisure.

1. Innovation can help people reach and surpass their targets, also in this quarter. The kind of innovation we have talked about in this book doesn't involve big, hairy, Noble-Prize-winning game changers. It is about simpler, faster, fairly low-risk ideas that can create better results for your business, here and now, or at least within a few quarters. If nothing else, your people should pursue innovation as usual because it can help them *win*.

2. Innovation can make people's jobs more fulfilling. With some luck, your employees already find their jobs enjoyable. Nonetheless, it has been remarkable to witness how innovation can make a difference to people's quality of life at work.

Make no mistake, innovation is *not* always a rose-scented tour of woo-woo land; it involves lots of failure and frustration as well. Yet most people we have worked with have found innovation to be a deep source of both energy and fulfillment. Jordan Cohen told us how the decision to create pfizerWorks had affected his life: "I am getting to do things that I never imagined I'd be able to do. It has stretched my leadership abilities, and I'm getting to try things and learn from those attempts and make changes so I can see things work. I rush to work every morning because of it. And I think my children have switched in thinking that 'work is something that you have to do,' to seeing their father have real joy at work. It has enriched all of our lives."

3. The ability to lead innovation is increasingly a consideration in promotion decisions. Despite what some innovation pundits may say, there will always be opportunities for people who *don't* innovate, provided they excel at business as usual. But more and more, companies are taking innovation seriously; in the survey we did with Capgemini, we found that in a single year (2011), the number of companies that employed a chief innovation officer rose from 33 percent to 42 percent. The increased corporate focus on innovation suggests that talented but noninnovative managers may see their career opportunities diminished by the ascendancy of leaders who master both business as usual *and* innovation as usual.

4. Innovation can make the world a better place. If you had lived in the thirteenth century, your children would have grown old and died in a world that looked almost exactly like that of their parents, except perhaps for the occasional bout of

plague or warfare. Despite the occasional downsides to our modern lifestyle, the past wasn't a particularly nice place to live; for instance, dentists didn't have anesthetics, people didn't have rights, and even kings and queens didn't have access to the kind of basic creature comforts that we have today. Innovation is worth doing because, through it, people can make the world and the workplace a better place to be.

NOTES

CHAPTER 1

5: *Gary Hamel and Bill Breen's book:* Gary Hamel with Bill Breen, *The Future of Management* (Boston: Harvard Business School Press, 2007); Julian Birkinshaw and Michael Mol, *Giant Steps in Management: Innovations That Change the Way You Work* (Upper Saddle River, NJ: FT Press/Prentice Hall, 2007).

5: *A great book on this is:* Constantinos C. Markides, *Game-Changing Strategies: How to Create New Market Space in Established Industries by Breaking the Rules* (San Francisco: Jossey Bass, 2008).

11: *You work with what Nudge authors:* Richard H. Thaler and Cass R. Sunstein, *Nudge: Improving Decisions About Health, Wealth, and Happiness* (New Haven, CT: Yale University Press, 2008).

12: *In their book Influencer:* Kerry Patterson, Joseph Grenny, David Maxfield, Ron McMillan, and Al Switzler, *Influencer: The Power to Change Anything* (New York: McGraw-Hill, 2007).

12: *For instance, as research into eating habits:* Brian Wansink, *Mindless Eating: Why We Eat More Than We Think* (New York: Bantam, 2006).

16: *Ideas aren't invented from scratch:* Andrew Hargadon, *How Breakthroughs Happen: The Surprising Truth About How Companies Innovate* (Boston: Harvard Business School Press, 2003).

17: *Prominent examples of open innovation:* A.G. Lafley and Ram Charan, *The Game-Changer: How You Can Drive Revenue and Profit Growth with Innovation* (New York: Crown Business, 2008).

18: *Steve Jobs's biography:* Walter Isaacson, *Steve Jobs* (New York: Simon & Schuster, 2011).

25: *The launch of pfizerWorks:* The full story (including Kreutter's quote) is described in our case study, "Jordan Cohen at pfizerWorks: Building the Office of the Future" (Barcelona, Spain: IESE Publishing, 2009).

25: *Cohen was featured in:* See for instance Jena McGregor, "Outsourcing Tasks Instead of Jobs," *BusinessWeek*, March 11, 2009; and Arianne Cohen, "Scuttling Scut Work," *Fast Company*, February 1, 2008.

29: *Models for innovative behavior:* For a recent example, see *The Innovator's DNA* by Jeff Dyer, Hal Gregersen, and Clayton Christensen (Boston: Harvard Business Review Press, 2011). Other examples are the various types of innovation audits.

31: *The sequential perspective on innovation:* Mark A. Runco, "Conclusions Concerning Problem Finding, Problem Solving, and Creativity," in *Problem Finding, Problem Solving, and Creativity*, ed. Mark A. Runco (New York: Ablex Publishing Corporation, 1994). A similar point is made by the authors of *The Innovator's DNA*.

CHAPTER 2

39: *Setting clear goals for innovation:* See for instance Kevin P. Coyne, Patricia Gorman Clifford, and Renée Dye, "Breakthrough Thinking from Inside the Box," *Harvard Business Review*, December 2007.

39: *According to a study we conducted:* Paddy Miller, Koen Klokgieters, Azra Brankovic, and Freek Duppen, "Managing Innovation: An Insider Perspective," April 2012. The full report is available on our web site, www.IAsUsual.com.

42: *A survey of 1,356 managers:* Jay Jamrog, Mark Vickers, and Donna Bear, "Building and Sustaining a Culture That Supports Innovation," *Human Resource Planning* 29, no. 3 (July 2006).

43: *The paradox of choice:* Barry Schwartz, *The Paradox of Choice: Why More Is Less* (New York: Ecco Press, 2003).

44: *Absent a specific problem statement:* See, for instance, Robert Cooper and Scott Edgett, "Ideation for Product Innovation: What Are the Best Methods?" *PDMA Visions Magazine*, March 2008.

46: *Innovation portfolios:* We recommend starting with Bansi Nagji and Geoff Tuff's article "Managing Your Innovation Portfolio," *Harvard Business Review*, May 2012, as well as Vijay Govindarajan and Chris Trimble's article "The CEO's Role in Business Model Reinvention," *Harvard Business Review*, January 2011.

CHAPTER 3

58: *Wheels on luggage:* Sadow's story is described in Joe Sharkey, "Reinventing the Suitcase by Adding the Wheel," *New York Times*,

October 4, 2010, as well as in an earlier article in the same newspaper. See Corey Kilgannon, "From Suitcases on Wheels to Tear-Free Onion Slicers," *New York Times*, August 6, 2000.

60: *For many years physiologists:* Edward de Bono, *New Think: The Use of Lateral Thinking in the Generation of New Ideas* (New York: Basic Books, 1968).

61: *Frans Johansson's books:* Frans Johansson, *The Medici Effect: Breakthrough Insights at the Intersection of Ideas, Concepts, and Cultures* (Boston: Harvard Business Press, 2004); and Frans Johansson, *The Click Moment: Seizing Opportunity in an Unpredictable World* (New York: Portfolio, 2012).

64: *The methods are from a study:* Robert Cooper and Scott Edgett: "Ideation for Product Innovation: What Are the Best Methods?" *PDMA Visions Magazine*, March 2008.

68: *Erich Joachimsthaler quote:* Personal conversation with Erich Joachimsthaler, September 9, 2012.

69: *Cooper and Edgett's study:* See http://www.stage-gate.net/downloads/working_papers/wp_29.pdf

69: *Rebecca Greenfield's article:* See http://www.theatlanticwire.com/technology/2012/07/google-doesnt-get-importance-gadget-packaging/54638/#.

72: *DSM's Powerpoint slides:* The DSM slides are available at http://www.slideshare.net/erikpras.

73: *Changing the office layout:* Anne-Laure Fayard and John Weeks, "Who Moved My Cube?" *Harvard Business Review*, July 2011.

74: *Julian Birkenshaw's book:* Julian Birkinshaw, *Reinventing Management: Smarter Choices for Getting Work Done* (San Francisco: Jossey-Bass, 2010).

CHAPTER 4

93: *Every consultant faces the temptation:* Ethan M. Rasiel and Paul N. Friga, *The McKinsey Mind: Understanding and Implementing the Problem-Solving Tools and Management Techniques of the World's Top Strategic Consulting Firm* (New York: McGraw-Hill, 2001).

101: *Henrik Werdelin quote:* Personal conversation with Henrik Werdelin, January 2012.

105: *As Pixar's president Ed Catmull:* Ed Catmull, "How Pixar Fosters Collective Creativity," *Harvard Business Review*, September 2008.

105: *After a session, it's up to the director:* Ibid.

CHAPTER 5

113: *Semmelweis and Klein:* The story of Semmelweis and his trials is thoroughly described in Sherwin Nuland, *The Doctors' Plague: Germs, Childbed Fever, and the Strange Story of Ignac Semmelweis* (New York: W. W. Norton & Company, 2004 reprint edition), as well as in Semmelweis's own account of his work, *Etiology, Concept, and Prophylaxis of Childbed Fever*, trans. K. Codell Carter (Madison, WI: University of Wisconsin Press, 1983).

117: *But as Rimer told us:* Personal conversation with David Rimer, February 2011.

118: *The problem was related:* Ibid.

120: *The research of Claudia Goldin and Cecilia Rouse:* Claudia Goldin and Cecilia Rouse, "Orchestrating Impartiality: The Impact of 'Blind' Auditions on Female Muscians," *American Economic Review* 90, no. 4 (September 2000): 715–741.

123: *Also, research by Tanya Menon and Jeffrey Pfeffer:* Tanya Menon and Jeffrey Pfeffer, "Valuing Internal vs. External Knowledge: Explaining the Preference for Outsiders," *Management Science* 49, no. 4 (April 2003).

127: *Maynard's article on General Motors:* Micheline Maynard, "At G.M., Innovation Sacrificed to Profits," *New York Times*, December 5, 2008.

132: *Kahneman's article on decision making:* Daniel Kahneman, "Don't Blink! The Hazards of Confidence," *New York Times*, October 19, 2011.

CHAPTER 6

137: *As the sociologist Everett M. Rogers:* Everett M. Rogers, *Diffusion of Innovations* Glencoe, IL: Free Press, 1962).

138: *As Bown puts it:* Stephen R. Bown, *Scurvy: How a Surgeon, a Mariner, and a Gentlemen Solved the Greatest Medical Mystery of the Age of Sail* (New York: St. Martin's Griffin, 2005).

138: *Gilbert Blane's story:* We published parts of the story of scurvy as a short article, "How a Snob Stopped Scurvy," in *IESE Insight*, Third Quarter, September 2012.

142: *Christian Budtz, coauthor of the book Storytelling:* Personal conversation with Christian Budtz.

143: *The ticking clock:* Scott Anthony, *The Little Black Book of Innovation: How It Works, How to Do It* (Boston: Harvard Business Review Press, 2011).

144: *As shown by Robert Cialdini:* See, for instance, Robert Cialdini's classic (and still worth reading) *Influence: The Psychology of Persuasion* (New York: Collins, 1993).

145: *In Influencer, a book that uses:* Kerry Patterson, Joseph Grenny, David Maxfield, Ron McMillan, and Al Switzler, *Influencer: The Power to Change Anything* (New York: McGraw-Hill, 2007).

150: *As a 2010 study by Jennifer S. Mueller:* Jennifer S. Mueller, Jack Goncalo, and Dishan Kamdar, "Recognizing Creative Leadership: Can Creative Idea Expression Negatively Relate to Perceptions of Leadership Potential?" *Journal of Experimental Social Psychology* 47 (2011): 494–498.

150: *Study on creativity training:* Ginamarie Scott, Lyle E. Leritz, and Michael D. Mumford, "The Effectiveness of Creativity Training: A Quantitative Review," *Creativity Research Journal* 16, no. 4 (2004).

CHAPTER 7

159: *Daniel Pink, in his book Drive:* Daniel H. Pink, *Drive: The Surprising Truth About What Motivates Us* (New York: Riverhead Hardcover, 2009).

159: *Importantly, though, research has shown:* See for instance Teresa Amabile and Steven Kramer's discussion of autonomy and clear goals in *The Progress Principle: Using Small Wins to Ignite Joy, Engagement, and Creativity at Work* (Boston: Harvard Business Review Press, 2011).

161: *His philosophy was simple:* Personal conversation with Marc Granger. Key details have been changed to maintain confidentiality.

161: *Granger described one instance:* Ibid.

164: *By addressing the worst passages:* One good read on this is Morten T. Hansen and Julian Birkinshaw, "The Innovation Value Chain," *Harvard Business Review*, June 2007.

165: *Consider this piece of advice:* Joachim Funke, "On the psychology of creativity," in Peter Meusburger, Joachim Funke, and Edgar Wunder (eds.), "Milieus of Creativity: An Interdisciplinary Approach to Spatiality of Creativity," *Knowledge and Space* 2, Springer Science + Business Media, 2009.

167: *In one of his papers, Sternberg:* Robert J. Sternberg, "The Nature of Creativity," *Creativity Research Journal* 18, no. 1 (2006).

167: *In another paper:* Robert J. Sternberg, "Domain-Generality Versus Domain-Specificity of Creativity," in Peter Meusburger, Joachim Funke, and Edgar Wunder (eds.), "Milieus of Creativity: An Interdisciplinary Approach to Spatiality of Creativity," *Knowledge and Space* 2, Springer Science + Business Media, 2009.

168: *One of the research subjects:* Gina Colarelli O'Connor, Andrew Corbett, and Ron Pierantozzi, "Create Three Distinct Career Paths for Innovators," *Harvard Business Review*, December 2009.

APPENDIX C

193: *Jordan Cohen told us:* Personal conversation with Jordan Cohen, 2009.

INDEX

ACKNOWLEDGMENTS

Some time ago, on one of those beautiful days Barcelona has lots of, we sat in an office at IESE Business School and decided to put our ideas into writing. At that point, Paddy had already published a book called *Mission Critical Leadership*, which had taken him one year to write. Since we were two people, we figured this book would take us *half* a year to write.

That, dear reader, is not how the arithmetic of book writing works. This book is a fully shared intellectual work, born of our long collaboration and fathered by both of us in equal measure. However, we are far from its only authors. Like the innovations we have described in these pages, our ideas have been brought to life, over a long period of time, through the creative spaces we have been fortunate enough to be immersed in. Below, in more or less random order, we have listed the many people who together formed the social and professional architecture that allowed us to write this book. Obviously, if any mistakes made it into these pages, ~~these are the people you should blame~~ we alone are responsible.

THE MANAGERS. First and foremost, this book would not have been possible without all those managers who, over the years, kindly allowed us to take part in their daily lives, letting us see how they went about making innovation happen. Many of these managers have become good friends, and several contributed to this book with ideas of their own: Jordan Cohen at Pfizer, Duncan Newsome at Diageo, Rory Simpson at Telefónica, Michael Campbell at the Dana Corporation, David Rimer at Index Ventures, Rich Raimundi, Paul Jeremaes, and Christine Pillon at HP, Karen Morris at Chartis Insurance, Glenn Rogers at Go Travel, Tricia Kullis at Puig, and the many others we can't mention by name (but you know who you are).

We owe a special thanks to Henrik Werdelin from Prehype, who in many ways coauthored the ideas and concepts in this book. If we had to point to a live role model for innovation architects and radical thinkers alike, it would be Henrik.

THE COLLEAGUES. Looking at our own architecture of innovation, we recognize that IESE Business School has made all the difference. First and foremost, our dean, Jordi Canals, provided unwavering support for the book, matched only by his patience as the writing and editing slouched glacially toward completion. Eric Weber, Frederic Sabrià, Giuseppe Auricchio, Mireia Rius, Mike Rosenberg, Pedro Videla, and M. Isabel de Muller also provided crucial support at various stages of the process.

Our thinking was continually inspired by the work of our fellow scholars of innovation: Josep Valor, Tony Dávila, Sandra Sieber, Joaquim Vilà, Bruno Cassiman, Fabrizio Ferraro, Magda Rosenmöller, Julia Prats, Alejandro Lago, Victor Martínez de Albéniz, Evgeny Káganer, Jan Simon, Marco Tortoriello, Pedro Nueno, and José Luis Nueno. Marta Elvira, Carlos Sanchez-Runde, Brian O'Connor Leggett, Max Torres, and our other colleagues in the department of Managing

People in Organizations provided an always stimulating collegial environment, as did Wim den Tuinder, Luise Zinke, Berit Dencker, Mark Wuyten, David Zorn, Idunn Jónsdóttir, Sylvia Johansson, Katherine Semler, Megan Shapleigh, and all the other great people at IESE. We're also grateful to IESE's teams of corporate entrepreneurs around the world, not least Kip Meyer, Paul Gallagher, Rich Sabreen, Begoña de Ros Raventós, and Elisabeth Boada in New York; Andreas Bernhardt and Christoph Burger at ESMT in Berlin; and the team at the China Europe International Business School (CEIBS): Pablo Fernandez, Juan Antonio Fernandez, Rama Velamuri, Hobbs Liu, and Claudia Lin. A special thanks goes to Azra Brankovic, our tireless research associate, Susana Minguell Moya-Angeler, whose expertise was invaluable, and Pilar Pallas Sanchez, who kept us sane and smiling throughout the process.

THE AGENT. Esmond Harmsworth, literary agent extraordinaire, took on our rough book proposal and steered us though several careful rounds of revision, patiently guiding us as we hammered our core ideas into a coherent whole. Along with Joanne Wyckoff, Caryn Levin, and the rest of his team at Zachary Shuster Harmsworth, Esmond proved to be an invaluable companion to the publishing process: helping us shape our ideas, deftly handling the occasional complication, and generally being a voice of reason, support, and whispered humorous asides. We consider ourselves uniquely lucky in getting an agent like Esmond, who not only understands publishing, but who also possesses a deep personal understanding of innovation and could help us elucidate our core ideas.

THE PUBLISHER. Together with Esmond Harmsworth and Henrik Werdelin, our editor Melinda Merino from Harvard Business Review Press is the "Fifth Beatle" of this book. The invisible editorial hand behind *Blue Ocean Strategy* and many other best-sellers, Melinda not only believed in our book's potential—she helped us realize that potential, spending countless hours working with us on the manuscript. Melinda's constructive feedback and spot-on suggestions for improvements, garnished with generous helpings of praise and humor, made the editing process a pleasure and was supremely helpful in clarifying and condensing our ideas.

We also benefited tremendously from the detailed comments of four innovation experts—Scott Anthony of Innosight, Julian Birkinshaw of London Business School, Alberto Colzi, and Astrid Sandoval—who kindly agreed to review our manuscript and provide feedback on it. We are very grateful for their insightful comments and suggestions, which proved to be of crucial value as we worked on improving the book.

Finally, Melinda's extended team at Harvard—Courtney Cashman, Erin Brown, Elizabeth Baldwin, Sally Ashworth, Jennifer Waring, Stephani Finks, Nina Nocciolino, Tracy Williams, Mary Dolan, John Wynne, Audra Longert, David Champion, and Jane Gebhart—made the entire process a pleasure to be part of and handled our occasional eccentricities with grace and humor. Together, they form one of the most capable, professional, well-oiled teams the publishing world has to offer.

THE SUPPORTERS. Besides the above-mentioned names, a small army of people helped us along the way. Astrid Sandoval's keen intellect helped shape our nascent ideas, and her advice played a critical role in the publishing process. Christoffer Lorenzen's razor-sharp mind provided us with numerous new insights for the book. Casper Willer's deep understanding of creativity and branding gave us new perspectives on our own thinking. Christian Budtz's unique eye for strategic creative communication took the book to a new level. Anders Ørjan Jensen's perspectives on organizational *realpolitik* made us understand the need for a different approach to innovation. Luciana Silvestri of Harvard Business School lent us her incandescent mind and omnibus-like knowledge of the academic literature. Café G in Copenhagen and Berkli Parc café in New York, run by Mark Hernandez and Brook Harkavy Hernandez, provided the perfect writing environments. Andy Cairns, Mark Turrell, Silvia Bellezza, Koen Klokgieters, Freek Duppen, Robert Christofferson, David Collis, Steven Dean, Anne Skare Nielsen, Bruce MacDonald, Harris Gordon, Mike Bayler, Tanya Carr-Waldron, Seth Appel, Agathe Blanchon-Ehrsam, Nick Hahn, Tammy Tan, Mike McCready, Jack Coyne, Steven Poelmans, Erin McCloy, and Bo Kousgaard all provided pieces of the puzzle. A number of friends gave us input on very early drafts, including Ann Akari Kohatsu, Sophie Jourlait-Filéni, Juliaan Bol, Rasmus Vendler Toft, Pooja Midha, and Jonas Heide Smith. Lise Lauridsen and John Sheeley provided peace of mind.

A special thanks goes to the members of the Danish mafia, who provided help with everything from content suggestions to general strategic and emotional support: Philip Petersen, Julie Paulli Budtz, Maria Fiorini, Metter Walter Werdelin, Ulrik Trolle, Peter Heering, Hans Werdelin, Marie Kastrup, Johan Frøshaug, Cecilie Muus Willer, Marcus Knuth, Simon Schultz, Birgit Løndahl, Niels Jørgen Engel, Lisbet Borker, Mik Strøyberg, Anna Frellsen, Flemming Fog, Gritt Løschenkohl, and the world's best godfather, Mikael Olufsen.

A very special thanks is owed to Erich Joachimsthaler, who helped us take the first critical step in our journey and who has been a constant source of advice, support, and good ideas throughout the process. Erich, thanks for all the inspiration.

THE FAMILY. Last but not least, if there was a Nobel prize for loving patience, our two families would surely have received it multiple times. None of this would have been possible without Sara, Sebastian, Georgina, Gitte, Henrik, Gregers, Merete, Clara, Carl-Johan, and Arendse. We love you.

ABOUT THE AUTHORS

PADDY MILLER is professor of Managing People in Organizations at IESE Business School in Barcelona. A globally consulted expert on leadership and corporate culture, he has more than twenty-five years of experience working with large companies. He has worked with senior executives in organizations such as Nike, Lufthansa, Henkel, Bayer, L'Oréal, Boeing, Citi, and the World Bank, among many others. As a speaker, he has appeared at the World Business Forum, the World Innovation Forum, and *The Economist's* Talent Management Summit.

Besides his work at IESE and in the corporate world, Miller is a sought-after speaker for executive programs in the United States, Europe, and Asia, and has led executive education courses offered by the business schools of Harvard University, the University of Virginia, the University of Cape Town, and the China Europe International Business School in Shanghai.

Miller holds a PhD in management from IESE Business School and an MBA from the University of Cape Town in South Africa. He is the author of *Mission Critical Leadership* and has written more than thirty-five case studies. His work on globally distributed teams was awarded by the Academy of Management.

THOMAS WEDELL-WEDELLSBORG is a partner at The Innovation Architects, a management consulting firm in New York City. An expert in innovation and corporate creativity, he has worked with managers in nearly all parts of the globe, including China, India, Russia, Singapore, Britain, France, the United States, and his native country, Denmark. He has founded two start-ups in the new media space and serves as an adviser to BBC Worldwide Labs.

Wedell-Wedellsborg is a frequent corporate speaker and has delivered keynote addresses at events such as HP's Executive Summit, Johnson & Johnson's HCS Fall Leadership Meeting, and Egmont Group's Management Conference. He is also a lecturer at IESE Business School, where he teaches in various executive education programs. His research has been published in the *Financial Times* and *Harvard Business Review*.

Wedell-Wedellsborg holds an MBA from IESE Business School and an MA in media science and economics from the University of Copenhagen. Prior to his business career, he served for four years as an officer and infantry platoon commander with the Danish Royal Guards.

Contact the authors
For more information, visit the book's website at www.IasUsual.com. For speaking engagements or other inquiries, write to contact@iasusual.com.